KUNDALINI
MEDITATION
QUESTIONS & ANSWERS

Foreword by
Master Charles Cannon

Santosh Sachdeva

Yogi Impressions®

Yogi Impressions®

KUNDALINI MEDITATION
First published in India in 2010 by
Yogi Impressions Books Pvt. Ltd.
1711, Centre 1, World Trade Centre,
Cuffe Parade, Mumbai 400 005, India.
Website: www.yogiimpressions.com

First Edition, May 2010

Cover design: Priya Mehta

The information contained in this book is not intended
to serve as a replacement for professional medical advice.
Any use of the information in this book is at the reader's
discretion. The intent of the author is to offer information
to support your emotional and spiritual well being. However,
the author and the publisher assume no responsibility
for your actions based on this information. The author
does not recommend the self-management of health or
mental health problems. You should never disregard medical
advice, or delay in seeking it, because of something you
have learned in this book.

ISBN 978-81-88479-66-5

Printed at: Repro India Ltd., Mumbai

Dedicated
with love and gratitude to
my Guru and Guide, the late
Justice M. L. Dudhat.

CONTENTS

Master Charles Cannon
Founder of the
Synchronicity Foundation
and originator of the
Synchronicity Meditative Experience.

FOREWORD

Many years ago, during a visit to Mumbai, India, I met Santosh Sachdeva in person. I had known her for several years through her children and had interacted with her in relation to her books on Kundalini. Meeting Santosh in person validated my distant experience of her. She radiated a unified presence, the hallmark of fully actualised Kundalini experience. Her writings are the outcome of many years of Kundalini experience – from initial awakening through the resultant, progressive process of ever-increasing, integrative wholeness.

Santosh is also a lovely woman who selflessly shares her experience and serves as a guide for many on the evolving path of Kundalini Yoga. I am thus honoured to write this Foreword to this book of questions and answers about Kundalini culled from her experience of many years.

My guru, Swami Muktananda Paramahansa, was a Kundalini adept. For twelve years, he personally trained me in the art and science of Kundalini Yoga. He often reminded me that while it was relatively easy to awaken Kundalini energy, it was the mark of the master to guide it to its culmination in substantiated wholeness, or the experience of unified consciousness. Santosh validates this time-honoured principle as she masterfully guides her students through this intricate and transformative journey.

It is further stated, in the classical tradition of Kundalini Yoga, that the authentic Kundalini master must fulfil specific qualifications. First, he or she must be substantiated in the state of unified consciousness which is validated by their holistic presence. Secondly, their unified state of being must serve as the empowerment that awakens and guides the Kundalini energy in their disciples. And thirdly, they must be thoroughly trained under the empowering guidance of a Kundalini guru, and thoroughly knowledgeable about all aspects of the evolving Kundalini experience. In my humble opinion, Santosh Sachdeva thoroughly fulfils all these qualifications as is evidenced not only in her writings, but also in the very living of her daily life and her interactions with those she empowers, awakens and guides.

In this modern world, there are many would-be gurus, some half-baked and some hardly baked at all. True and authentic masters are rare indeed.

As you read these rich pages, you will encounter a true and authentic master of Kundalini experience. I encourage you to be grateful for what you have found, and to celebrate your most fortunate experience. It is said that when the student is ready, the master comes. If you are reading this book, you are ready. Now, simply open yourself to the authentic master who has come. In doing so, you will come to know Santosh Sachdeva as the adept that she is and you will inevitably love her, as do I, for all that she embodies and so selflessly shares.

It is said that the true guru is the one who takes you from the darkness of ignorance into the light of truth. It is my sincere hope that you will flower within this experience, and come to know Santosh by the name I have given her... Mataji... which means... Dear Mother. May Mataji Santosh Sachdeva shower you with her many blessings while you are reading this most masterful book.

Master Charles Cannon
H. H. Swami Vivekananda Saraswati
April 2010

INTRODUCTION

Since the release of *Conscious Flight into the Empyrean*, *Kundalini Diary*, and *Kundalini Awakening*, three of my books that form *The Kundalini Trilogy*, there has been a constant flow of questions regarding the mystery of Kundalini; how it works and the risks involved in practising Kundalini meditation and yoga. Some readers sent in letters and emails while others came over in person to discuss their doubts and to seek clarifications.

I found it surprising that it was mostly young people between twenty-five and forty years of age who appeared to be awakening to the changes and the stirrings taking place within them. Somewhat confused and ignorant of what has happening, the first person they approached was their doctor, and sometimes, a psychiatrist.

There was a young lady who had attended a Chakra Workshop some years ago, which had led to constant headaches and other physical problems. She had visited several doctors but they could not offer any solution. The only advice I could give her was to go back to the group that had conducted the Workshop and seek their guidance. If properly guided, she would be alright.

In another instance, I remember how shocked I was when a girl from Germany who came to meet me mentioned that a doctor had put her on a course of medicines because of the nature of the experiences she had begun to have. It was quite clear to me that in reality what she was experiencing was an aspect of Kundalini awakening. In another instance, a young lady who had returned from a yoga session she had attended at some spa found to her horror that each time she would start to meditate, she began to make peculiar sounds. Another young man experienced a premature opening of his Ajna chakra. In each of these cases, the energy had been disturbed and not guided. As a result, the symptoms that were being manifested were not being effectively relieved by medical intervention.

People who have read *The Kundalini Trilogy* have responded in their own unique way. For some, the books have helped them to awaken to a new experience without the fear that is generally associated with Kundalini awakening. Others who experienced strange and inexplicable sensations realised that a certain awakening was happening and they had to seek guidance. There were still others who identified with the illustrations in each of the books in the Trilogy and began to understand that though they were going through an experience that was out of the ordinary, there was an explanation for what was transpiring with them. They felt validated and reassured.

This book endeavours to provide answers based on my experience and understanding of the working of Kundalini meditation and awakening. You may relate to some aspect of this book, a question, or experiences similar to those being discussed. Hopefully, these answers will help you on your spiritual journey.

I have also included extracts of talks given by Master Charles Cannon, an American mystic and disciple of Siddha Yoga Master, Swami Muktananda Paramahansa. These comments should provide a contemporary understanding of the subject.

It is assumed that the reader who has picked up this book is at some stage of Kundalini awakening and is looking for reassurance or for answers that will guide the process of awakening. If so, you will find your answer in some section or the other of this book.

Finally, I would like to encourage everyone who is experiencing inexplicable symptoms that cannot be addressed by science to seek a guide or someone who can explain what is transpiring. Through meditation, you can be guided on your journey within. Once you begin to understand the process, the symptoms will disappear and you will experience an opening to another dimension.

My best wishes are with you.

PRANA

What is prana?

Prana is that substance in the air from which all life has emanated. It is both macrocosmic and microcosmic. Because prana is part of the air and atmosphere, we are constantly breathing it in. However, when we speak of prana, we do not mean breath, air or oxygen, but rather the original life force which is everywhere, pervading all existence – animate and inanimate.

Prana is visualised as a misty, cloud-like flow of energy so subtle in form that it is undetectable by scientific methods. In the physical body, prana flows like an electric current through an intricate pathway of subtle nerves called *nadis*. "The cosmic manifestation of prana in the individual body is represented by Kundalini," says Swami Niranjanananda Saraswati.

How will the practice of pranayama help me in my daily life?

Firstly, it is important to understand what is meant by the practice of *pranayama*. The simple act of breathing in and out is an involuntary process, whereas in the practice of pranayama you consciously direct prana throughout the body. Therefore, the benefits you derive will be felt at all levels and you will create a balance between your physical, mental and emotional bodies. Your organs will function better, your circulation will improve, your respiratory system will work better and you will feel more relaxed and energetic.

As you progress in your practice, you will find that your awareness levels are much higher and you are now better able to deal with challenging situations. You will be less prone to mood swings. Instead, there will be a realisation that there is a definite purpose behind every thought, action and deed.

If and when pranayama becomes a part of your daily life, then, with the purification of your whole personality you will, in due course, achieve a state of fixed concentration and an expansion of consciousness which, in turn, will lead to spiritual awakening.

Can Kundalini be awakened by practising pranayama?

Pranayama is not just a breath-control technique or a means to increase prana in the body. If followed correctly, and in the sequence prescribed, it can prove to be a powerful method to awaken dormant energy. Swami Niranjanananda Saraswati explains the process:

"Prana is the inward moving force which is said to create a field moving upwards from the navel to the throat. *Apana* is the outward moving force which is said to create a field moving downwards from the navel to the anus. Both prana and apana move spontaneously in the body, but they can be controlled through yogic practices. The Upanishads say a method has to be employed to reverse the direction of the oppositely moving forces of prana and apana so that they unite with *samana* in the naval centre. The result of these forces coming together is the awakening of Kundalini."

If you want to know the process of change that pranayama and yoga bring about, you have to experiment with the technique and try to understand the energy and structure of the change process – the Kundalini. To shift or alter the state of consciousness, both the mental and physical bodies must be stimulated and coordinated. This is why every meditation and kriya has a mantra. The kriya stimulates the physical body while the mantra directs the activated energy.

When a spiritually evolved aspirant is regular in the practice of pranayama and his/her diet is light, the awakening of Kundalini may take place. When starting on such an endeavour, it is advisable that an aspirant restricts his/her diet to fruits and juices for a specified period of time. With this preparation the awakening can be rapid. If there is a flaw in the practice, then the results can be harmful. This is why any programme dealing with

Kundalini should be studied under the guidance of an experienced teacher so that, if the need arises, an aspirant would be able to clear any of his/her doubts and move on confidently.

I have been practising pranayama and meditation for a number of years. Some months ago I had participated in a Chakra Workshop. Since then, when I sit for meditation, I feel something stirring in my body. I am quite afraid. How should I handle this?

Because you have been meditating, the workshop has probably activated the dormant energy within you which is rising upwards. It is crucial that you bring this to the notice of your guru. If you don't have one, then you should go back to the person who conducted the Chakra Workshop and ask for guidance. You could either discontinue your practice and get on with your life or you could become regular with your practice. Begin by fixing a time and place for meditation because once the energy starts to move upwards, the physical, mental and emotional bodies will undergo several changes. You must exercise complete surrender. Do not resist the energy. Let go of yourself completely and float along with the current. Higher forces have taken over, you need not worry.

With the upward movement of the Kundalini many unexpected things may happen because you are now moving into the region of the unknown. Do not be afraid, things will unfold as you go along with your practice. At this stage, any resistance is liable to create problems and can prove to be harmful. If possible, get in touch with someone who has been through the Kundalini experience or talk to like-minded people who are going through a similar process. Remember, if there is even an ounce of fear, either discontinue your *sadhana* or consult the person who had conducted the workshop.

What is meant by the term 'subtle bodies'?

'Subtle bodies' is a term used for psycho-spiritual bodies, each corresponding to a subtle plane of existence in a sequence that culminates in the physical form, moving outward, from invisible to visible. The subtle body is that part of our being in which we experience our thoughts and emotions. It is made up of light and energy and cannot be seen with the physical eyes. It is usually described as an oval halo of shimmering light that surrounds the physical body. In the scriptures it is defined as *Panch Kosha*.

The subtle body comprises of the mind, intellect, ego, accumulated impressions, *jnanendriyas* (subtle aspect of the senses), *karamendriyas* (subtle aspect of the organs of action) and the pranic body comprised of five pranas (the five vital airs); *prana, apana, samana, udana* and *vyana*.

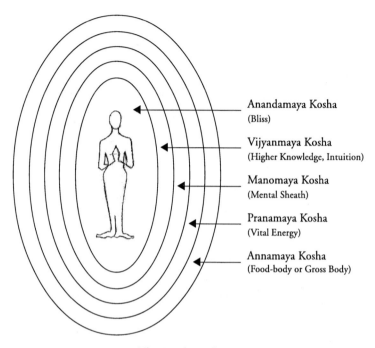

Anandamaya Kosha
(Bliss)

Vijyanmaya Kosha
(Higher Knowledge, Intuition)

Manomaya Kosha
(Mental Sheath)

Pranamaya Kosha
(Vital Energy)

Annamaya Kosha
(Food-body or Gross Body)

The Panch Koshas.

The human form is made up of five sheaths. Moving outward, from invisible to visible, from subtle to gross, these sheaths are:

- Anandamaya Kosha; a dimension of pure bliss.
- Vijyanmaya Kosha; the sheath of higher knowledge which manifests itself as intuition or insight.
- Manomaya Kosha; the dimension of mind which contains intellect, memory, concept and reason.
- Pranamaya Kosha which is composed of prana; the vital energy that activates the body and motivates the mind.
- Annamaya Kosha; the physical body, so called because it is dependent on *anna* – grain or gross food.

In simple terms, these sheaths of existence are said to be composed of bliss, intuition, intellect, energy and food.

All these dimensions of being interpenetrate and interact with each other. Each sheath is said to be composed of energy and the energy in each sheath has its own speed of vibration. In the physical sheath the energy vibration is slowest, though, as we move through the koshas the vibration becomes faster and finer until it once again resolves itself back to Pure Consciousness.

KUNDALINI

What is Kundalini shakti?

Kundalini shakti is the name given to the dormant energy lying at the root of the spine. It can be described as a storehouse of creative energy, the very foundation of our consciousness. When this force moves through our body, a change is brought forth in our consciousness. The initial awakening is only a starting point. The arousal can be quite dramatic and is traditionally understood as an intense process of purification that leads to transcendence of body and mind, culminating in the unification or oneness with Consciousness as Whole, which can be termed as God, Source Consciousness or Pure Consciousness.

Except in rare cases, it can take years for the body to be purified and ready enough to handle the high-powered voltage of a full-blown Kundalini awakening. In its unmanifested state, it is symbolised as a serpent coiled in three and a half circles. When it is ready to awaken and unfold, it ascends up the Sushumna (the subtle channel in the spinal cord) passing through the chakras, starting with the Mooladhara, then Swadhisthana, Manipura,

Anahata, Vishuddhi and Ajna chakras, and up to the Sahasrar centre where it unites with Pure Consciousness.

Is there any way to know whether I am ready for Kundalini experience?

If your physical, mental and emotional bodies are in balance, then you are ready for Kundalini awakening. This means that you are able to manage your mind in emotional conflicts. Ask yourself these questions: Are you tolerant? Are you able to take insults without reacting? Are you fearless? Are you able to endure ill-will, spite, hatred, greed, envy? Can you stay calm in the face of anger? If you can handle these and other such emotions with equanimity, then you are ready for Kundalini awakening and the subtle dimension of experience, provided you find the right guru.

The following note outlines the process of purification of the body and mind organism.

Master Charles Cannon on The Primary Trinity

When the primary trinity of the physical, mental and emotional dimensions are in balance, the subtle dimension actualises as witness consciousness, the detached observation of the relative field. Herein we are watching the physical, mental and emotional dimensions from the now dominant subtle dimension of witness consciousness. Yet, the mental dimension has several levels, and a complete detachment from them is a gradual process in meditation.

Firstly, there are the gross levels of data and interpretation. Then there are more subtle levels of mental impressions with less interpretation and data processing. As witness consciousness in the subtle dimension becomes more dominant and constant in meditation, there is complete detachment from all the levels of the mental dimension. Then there is just the observation of stillness. Remember, we meditate to be present... to simply watch the experience. By simply watching we extract our focus from the physical, mental and emotional dimensions and they progressively become still. Then we are watching stillness and it is then that we progress to more subtle states of pure awareness in the causal and supra causal dimensions.

What are the other experiences associated with the phenomenon of Kundalini? I have experienced strange sounds, light, heat, tingling, and tears running down my face for no reason. What transformations may or may not occur, and at what level?

An aspirant who is in the energy field of the guru and who meditates regularly may, in the course of his sadhana, experience various colours of lights such as yellow, red, orange, blue, green, indigo, purple or white. Sometimes, one experiences flashes of light. If you are sensitive and observant, you will be able to understand from which centre the experience is coming. You will be able to identify the chakra and know its attributes.

With the movement of energy, there can be experience at the physical, mental and emotional level. This can come in the form of trembling, sudden jerks, the feeling of ants crawling all over your body, a tingling sensation in the scalp, the rolling of your eyeballs, or your tongue may revert back or rise up towards the palate. You may experience fragrances. You could get locked in a posture and hear different kinds of *nad* (subtle sounds). All these experiences arise when the energy is moving through the subtle body meridians. When it encounters any resistance, there is a spasm in the subtle body meridian which is manifested one way or the other in the physical body. You may experience your body going up in flames and then see yourself as a heap of ashes or you may feel as though a snake is moving up in your body.

The body can get into different postures and you could go through different *kriyas*. If you feel you have stopped breathing, it is a sign of an active Kundalini. You may emit sounds like those of animals, birds, lions, dogs. This, too, is a sign of an awakened Kundalini.

As you progress on your path and purification of your subtle bodies occurs, you may experience a feeling of expansion. You may feel as if you are growing taller, or your mouth is opening wider or your limbs are twisting. All these are experiences of the subtle body.

In meditation, there are experiences from different levels of vibration, from the gross vibratory level to the subtle level of existence.

When there is a shift in your vibration, it means you have moved from one level of consciousness to another level of consciousness. If you are at a lower level, you may encounter entities of that vibratory level. No one likes an intruder in their space. Just as you feel threatened when an unknown person encroaches on your space, similarly, these entities can react and will use any means to scare you off. Do not panic at this stage, but take yourself away and move up to another vibratory level. These entities can do you no harm. They are of subtle vibration and can only attack your mind. If you are strong-minded and fearless, you can pass through unharmed. If, however, you are weak and fearful, then great damage can happen. The energy field of the guru is what will support you through the hazards that you may encounter on the way.

At the gross level of vibration you may encounter thought forms which can be repulsive, distorted, absurd and comic, with distorted figures and faces. These thought forms are all around us and are created in the course of our daily lives through the emotions let out because of bombings, rape, and violence. Pain, sorrow, fear, disgust, ill-will, spite, hatred, lust, greed, all take on a form and float or hover around. Anyone going through some form of sorrow will attract similar thought forms. As a result, his sorrow gets multiplied. If someone is having a fit of temper, his magnetic field at that moment will attract similar thought forms and his temper can turn into a rage. Similarly, hatred can turn into violence and so on. If during meditation you see these distorted thought forms and get fearful, that fear will attract similar thought forms and further add to your fear. In order to be able to move away from this lower vibratory level you have to evolve a keen sense of discrimination.

Once you have crossed this level successfully, then, each time there is a shift in vibration, you are moving to another subtler level. There will be the astral level, which according to my experience, resembles in all its aspects the physical level except it is subtle and not tangible. Thus consciousness will keep shifting depending on how you are progressing, because to shift the state of consciousness, both the physical and mental systems must be stimulated and coordinated to create a subtle change. The kriyas of the programme you are following code these particular combinations in an extremely subtle way and control how the various energy systems interlock. Each kriya produces a different effect. Some bring understanding, others create mental stability, some develop sensitivity and still others bring forth physical changes. Your journey will depend on how effective your practice is.

The experiences of the subtler levels cannot be put into words. You will have to undergo your own journey to experience it. If you want to know mine then you will find it described in *The Kundalini Trilogy*.

You may hear sounds which are not from the physical realm, they are the soundless sounds. The first sound is what I call the 'Chinnnnnnn' sound. Swami Muktananda of Ganeshpuri says that this is the sound of Consciousness.

With the purification of the subtle bodies, sensitivity increases and you may see or feel the vibration of the chakras or see or feel the energy flow from or to you.

Vibrations of the Vishuddhi and Swadhisthana chakra.

Each vibratory level offers its own challenges.

As you progress on your path and the dormant pathways open up, you may see new vistas or get glimpses of lives lived earlier.

Instead of just going through the experience, the endeavour should be to go deeper to find the source of all experience. Just don't pass off your experience as something meaningless. Every experience is a part of the whole that is your journey and goal.

The short notes below by Master Charles Cannon will provide a better understanding of tingling, lights and tears.

Tingling

The tingling 'electrical' that you experience is a reflex from the subtle body meridians into the connective tissue of the physical body. It is caused by a change in the frequency of vibration of the energy within the meridians. In each successive level of its course the frequency is decelerated and until you integrate this new frequency, it can be experienced as such.

Flashes of light

The flashes of light are experienced when the subtle dimensions become dominant in one's focus. In these dimensions, the oscillation of polarity within the field of relativity is so accelerated that awareness appears as a continuity. This is because the mind cannot cognise these subtle dimension polar oscillations. The frequency of vibration corresponds to the speed of light and, when the mind is momentarily activated, it cognises the experience of light. Again, you are perceiving from a multi-dimensional awareness which includes all dimensions simultaneously. It demonstrates constancy in witness consciousness.

Tears

This is associated with the clearing of the ocular meridians related to the third eye vortex. In the Kundalini traditions, it was referred to as appropriate purification. As the primary trinity – physical, mental and emotional – becomes more constant in balance, harmonic coherence results. With duration in harmonic coherence, the subtle dimensions actualise. The first of these dimensions is termed as the Subtle Dimension and relates to the third eye vortex. It is your harmonic frequency of vibration that is evolving. The associated meridians – as you actualise multi-dimensionally, generate reflexes that can produce tears. The result will be increased constancy in witness consciousness.

When I sit for meditation, I feel something gently moving up from the base of my spine. Is this the Kundalini?

Aspirants who are meditating regularly may feel the sensation of energy moving up the spine. In most cases, this is not the Kundalini energy moving up, but a release of pranic force that starts at the Mooladhara and moves up through the Pingla nadi, partially purifying the chakras, until it reaches the head where it is dispersed. This, however, can be a process of preparation for the eventual awakening of Kundalini, which may not be as gentle.

Is it possible for a person to awaken the Kundalini by practising Kundalini Yoga?

If a person awakens his Kundalini through yoga, and has no knowledge and understanding about what it entails, he could be heading for disaster. However, when it is awakened through the grace of the guru, that in itself will lead the Kundalini on the right path.

What is the difference between Kundalini and prana and how can one distinguish between them when they are manifested?

The force that supports creation in all its aspects is called prana. The universal prana is the cosmic energy that we draw in through the breath. The cosmic manifestation of prana in the individual body is represented by Kundalini shakti which lies dormant at the base of the spine.

28

How does the guru guide a disciple once the Kundalini awakens?

When the energy first awakened in me, my guru's first questions to me were: Did I have old parents or in-laws to take care of, and did I have young children who needed my attention? I understand now that these questions were essential because once you get on to the path of Kundalini, it requires your full attention or you have to have the rare ability to handle the mundane and spiritual simultaneously.

Once the guru ascertains that the Kundalini has awakened in an aspirant, then it is guided by him through means appropriate to the receptivity of an aspirant. It may be done through transmission of thought, through one-to-one dialogue where the guru clears an aspirant's doubts and allays his fears, or he may guide an aspirant by telling him when to slow down, when to stop and so forth.

Can Kundalini be awakened through any predominant chakra?

Yes, Kundalini can be awakened through any chakra predominant in an individual. This could happen in a person who has worked out his karma at different levels. If, for instance, he has worked through his karmas of the lower stages of lust, greed, jealousy, hate, lethargy etc., which are the expressions of the Mooladhara chakra, he will awaken at the Swadhisthana chakra in his next birth. At this chakra, there is no conscious activity or manifestation. Everything here exists in a potential state. Every experience, negative as well as positive, is recorded here. It is the home of the unconscious. When the Kundalini is resting in the Swadhisthana chakra, all the negative *samskaras* (accumulated impressions), karmas and sexual desires rise to the surface and, once we have worked through them, which may take several lifetimes, the Kundalini will move on to the Manipura chakra. The Manipura chakra is the centre of dynamism, energy, will power and achievement. Once the Kundalini has reached this chakra, and if a person leads a balanced life, the Kundalini will not move back to the lower chakras. With the guidance of a guru, the person would then pursue a higher purpose and in the future the Kundalini would move on to higher levels.

Can mantras, and massage with special preparation of oils, ghee etc., help in the process of awakening? Can the process of shuddhi, basti as practised in Ayurveda or Yoga be of any help?

Yes, mantras and massage, *shuddhi* and *basti* can be of great help. Shuddhi and basti help in the purification of the body while the massage helps activate the energy and the mantras give it direction. When an aspirant goes in for any of the above, he first needs to understand the implications of the massage and the mantras. If it is implied that it is to activate the energy centres within, one should be wary and first determine whether the teacher has enough experience to be able to channelise the energy.

What is the benefit of Kundalini awakening for the general public?

One awakened person can change the lives of people around him. The sages have said that if even one person in a family awakens, it affects seven future generations. We can see the transformation happening at the level of the masses under the auspices of the spiritual leaders today. The transformation is taking place on a massive scale and a shift is being created in human consciousness. This shift happens at an unconscious level through the teaching. The gurus or masters deal with their devotees as they would deal with children. Through their discourses and public interaction, they impart knowledge that purifies the intellect and motivates people to follow the noble path. Their teachings help to move away from superstition and adopt a more pragmatic and positive approach to the situations of life.

Adepts appear in this world to guide people in the proper way of living and to lead them on the right path. The yogis also believe that each time a person awakens every single rock, plant, insect, bird or animal gets a boost in evolution. So it is a step forward in consciousness.

If one does not feel the energy moving, does it mean the Kundalini is not awakened?

An aspirant who has been practising a form of pranayama and meditation for some years will, through the practice, have created a free-flow of prana through the subtle body meridians. Such an aspirant may not feel the energy moving. Individuals on the *Bhakti Marg* also may not feel the movement of Kundalini because they operate from unconditional love and devotion and will not face hazards of Kundalini.

Similarly, there are masters who through lifetimes of sadhana have reached a stage where energy flows through them freely. In another aspirant, a breathing technique may have a sudden impact and the dormant energy lying coiled at the base of the spine may be jolted from its resting place. In such an eventuality, the physical, mental and emotional bodies of the aspirant may not be ready for the sudden arousal of Kundalini. Such an aspirant will feel the workings of Kundalini, because the balance that is brought about by meditation and pranayama is taken over by the Kundalini. If this happens, then the aspirant has a very interesting and challenging journey ahead.

What can cause Kundalini shakti to get active?

Kundalini can awaken naturally as one goes through the different stages of life. If one lives a well-balanced life, then at every stage the Kundalini will support the individual as it would find a relatively clear pathway through the chakras. This would be termed as a natural awakening of the Kundalini shakti. Kundalini can also be awakened through the recitation of specific mantras, breathing techniques (pranayama), and yoga techniques. The shakti can further be awakened through shaktipat or grace of the guru. Shaktipat can be given by a mere glance, word, or touch of the guru. It can happen while he is present or absent. In order to absorb this experience the aspirant needs nerves of steel, for this is the process of dismantling the old data and creating the new.

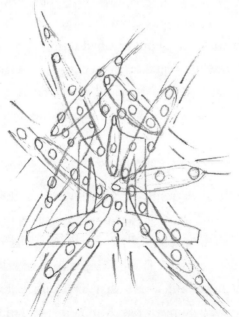

The subtle body, with the awakening of Kundalini, goes into a flux that causes rearrangement of atoms.

When shakitpat happens, the physical body undergoes changes. Its cells become charged and rejuvenated. A process of complete transformation is set in motion.

Depending on the psyche of an aspirant, if Kundalini becomes active, an aspirant can be faced with fear, anxiety, awe or wonder. If one has an adventurous spirit and is fearless by nature then the journey can be exciting and exhilarating for there is nothing mundane about it.

What does shaktipat mean?

Shaktipat means the transmission of energy between guru and disciple. The guru does not do anything, just his presence is enough. He becomes a catalytic agent for a seeker who has attained some depth in meditation. The guru serves as a channel to regulate the energy in relation to the aspirant's capacity to withstand the force of transmission; otherwise it can cause a breakdown of the nervous system.

Does shaktipat and grace mean one and the same thing?

Though the end result of both events is the same, the process is different. Shaktipat requires a guru as the transmitter and a spiritually evolved *shishya* as the receiver.

When an aspirant is following a path of self-surrender; when he/she is not aware that anything is to happen – does not even know what Kundalini is – then in such a state of receptivity, grace may descend like lightning.

The impact and the result is the same as shaktipat, in fact, it is a form of shaktipat, but straight from the heavens. There is no medium needed for the grace to descend except a state of receptivity in an aspirant.

Does one get enlightened after shaktipat?

No. Shaktipat works like a flash of lightning that lights your path. It gives you a glimpse of the road ahead. With shaktipat, your energy and hidden potential will surface and the rate of growth and expansion will intensify. The flash of lightning will have illumined your path and you will move ahead with trust and confidence for you have had the glimpse of what lies ahead. Shaktipat has shown you the way but you must travel the road alone.

Is shaktipat related to the mind?

No, shaktipat is not associated with the mind. It is an energetic exchange between the guru and the disciple. The explosive exchange creates a shift in the energy structure of the disciple – the atoms are rearranged in one stroke. It is like a jigsaw puzzle being dismantled and rearranged to allow space for the shift in *chitta-shakti* (consciousness) that is the result of shaktipat. In shaktipat *deeksha*, the disciple receives the support of the guru's energy, and not his mind. After establishing contact with the consciousness of the disciple, the consciousness of the guru returns to him.

During Shaktipat, the old psyche is shattered to make way
for the new one to manifest.

The rest of the disciple's spiritual journey that follows
the awakening of Kundalini will be manifest in accordance
with the accumulated impressions of the disciple.

*I am a cranio-sacral therapist. A client of mine, who is
a yoga teacher, went through intense physical movement
on the treatment table. It started with undulations of
the spine and arching of the back, and went on to lifting
of hips, legs, and turning from side to side. She felt very
light and somewhat tired towards the end. Would this be
a manifestation of Kundalini?*

When one is practising a form of Kundalini Yoga, there is a word that describes the movements your patient is making or manifesting. The word is kriya and it means movement. In the contemporary idiom, it is meridian spasm. It indicates that the meridians are not able to dilate enough to allow an unrestricted flow of energy; therefore, some resistance is created and the spasm in the meridian reflexes into the physical body, and is experienced as shaking, twitching or jerking. If yogic postures are being formed or emulated, they will be very fluid and graceful, occurring almost in slow motion. There would be no feeling of tiredness, unless physical effort is unconsciously being exerted.

You have had extraordinary experiences and I have read your record of all you went through. How has your life changed after your experience of awakening?

It is not life that changes after the awakening; it is a change that takes place within oneself. When awakening happens or, in other words when Kundalini moves, our body and consciousness change with it. Transformation does not occur overnight, it is rather a process of gradual change that occurs by being in the energy field of the guru, and the interaction that occurs between guru and disciple.

This also means that one is always aware of the messages coming, directly or indirectly, through the guru. Awareness will lead to understanding, and understanding will lead to acceptance. When you can accept yourself, all your limitations, insecurities, and fears will fade away. They will be replaced with abundance, wisdom, and hope. If the teaching is practised with respect and reverence, it will change your life. You will experience freedom from past relationships and move into an expanded state of consciousness.

Each one of us will respond and imbibe the teaching according to our psyche and need. The lessons I learnt are:

One: Not to avoid situations in life or even in myself, but to learn to accept them and know their nature. This would require a state of mind that is continuously observing the nature of events in order to develop the ability to see the reality behind situations that are different from what appears to be, and to look at things in their positive as well as negative aspect.

Two: I have learnt not to jump to conclusions but to look at things from the other's perspective. We have all come with our own scripts and the ways in which the drama of our life should unfold. Unfortunately, very few scripts play out the way we have planned they should. So, the better person is one who has the awareness to pick up the cue that the other's dialogue offers and gives an appropriate response. This requires one to be present in the moment and always alert. I have learnt not to judge, complain or blame, and to accept everything as is.

The change is not only being experienced in my life, I can see it reflected in my childrens' lives also. They are living their life in awareness. The sages have said that when one person in a family gets on the spiritual path – the grace is experienced by seven generations. I can well believe that, for when a change in consciousness occurs in one person in a family, his/her language, action and behaviour would invite a similar response.

I have heard people narrate experiences of Kundalini even though they do not have a guru nor follow any Kundalini technique. How is this possible?

These days there are various workshops being conducted on yoga, pranayama, chakras and the mass awakening of the Kundalini. Such activities can produce a premature awakening and, if the teacher is not equipped to guide the awakened energy, it can prove to be harmful at the physical, mental and emotional levels.

Normally, a guru is essential for the awakening of the Kundalini. In rare cases, the awakening may happen due to past samskaras during which a person has probably practised some form of sadhana. So, at an appropriate time in this life, the symptoms of Kundalini are manifest to lead that individual to his next level of growth. In this situation if the individual can surrender, then the Kundalini itself becomes the guru. However, even in this situation, the person instead of getting confused and groping in the dark will have to seek the mentorship of a living guru who can provide guidance.

If I am following a course in Kundalini Yoga, do I have to adopt a particular lifestyle and diet?

When I went through the experience of awakening, my guru did not ask me to make any changes in my life or food habits. I still went about my daily business. What is required is purity of thought, clarity of mind and a pure consciousness. You may have thoughts about purity, generosity, compassion or charity but in the unconscious of your personality there may be conflicts and unresolved issues. Once the Kundalini is awakened and moves, it will bring all stored data to the surface. If your personality is full of obsessions and mental blocks, then you can have a problem. Therefore, before embarking on Kundalini awakening you should undergo a process of thought purification and an understanding of your deeper self. You should be conscious of your negative thought processes and resolve such issues because, with the awakening of Kundalini, a process of transformation will start.

In your book Kundalini Awakening you have a visual with an inverted illustration of a jug pouring milk into a bowl. Does this have any meaning?

The illustration you write about is given below. For me it symbolised the Kundalini energy flowing in one stream from Ajna chakra into the Sahasrar. The scriptures have also described this experience as the 'turning of the lotus cup on the moon', as seen in the other illustration. In this visual is seen the light of the Ajna chakra shaped like a crescent moon with the inverted vibrations of the lotus or Sahasrar centre.

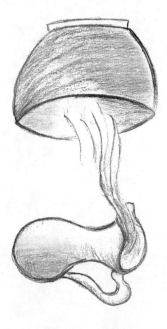 

Inverted jug and a bowl.   The inverted lotus over the moon.

The experience is symbolic and indicates the coming into balance of the Ajna chakra and Sahasrar, thus indicating the changes taking place in the subtle body as the aspirant progresses on the path of self-discovery, moving towards a clear development of the direct power of thought.

The awakening of Kundalini is, invariably, a powerful experience. If you have my book *Conscious Flight into the Empyrean*, you will find illustrations that depict the different aspects of Kundalini.

MEDITATION

What is the purpose of meditation?

In meditation, we go through the process of introspection, perception and negation. This means that if a negative thought surfaces, we observe it and let it pass. This is the preliminary process of purification in an aspirant, which involves his physical, mental and emotional bodies. In this way, the purification of thought takes place at conscious, subconscious, and unconscious levels.

The subconscious level is a storehouse of unfulfilled desires, unresolved experiences, and hurtful incidents that have sunk deep into the personality and are lying dormant, ready to surface as a defense mechanism in the form of an action-reaction situation. The unconscious is composed of impulses, instincts and moods that are totally unknown to us in the moment. They will surge up to express themselves under provocative conditions.

In what way does meditation help an aspirant on the path of spiritual unfolding?

In meditation, when the conscious mind becomes

quiet, the subconscious and unconscious get a chance to float up. It is during this period of stillness, when the conscious mind is not alert, that immoral, hateful, and cruel thoughts start gushing out, and the seeker is horrified and unable to believe and comprehend the underlying viciousness of his personality. If at this stage an aspirant does not get involved, does not go into a fear mode, stays balanced and remains the observer of what is surfacing, then all the repressed negative thoughts, when they surface at a conscious level, will disappear, never to return again.

This is a crucial stage in an aspirant's journey because once the floodgates are opened, the aspirant has no chance of escaping being swept away. If he can stand apart from the upsurge of emotions, the flow shall, in time, end of its own accord. By meditation, the mind will be emptied of its subconscious data. Once the cravings, desires and passions that caused the illusory pains in life roll off, he will experience peace within and without. The conscious mind, released from the pressures of the subconscious, becomes lighter and moves into the subtler dimension of meditative experience.

Finally, through the process of meditation, an aspirant consciously withdraws his attention from the external world and moves towards the discovery of the self.

Sometimes, when meditating, I see a snake moving up in my body or ants crawling all over my body. What does this mean?

Shakti can move in any way it chooses. As it becomes active it can be felt as an energetic force, taking the aspirant by surprise. Its movement can be felt as a steady stream up the spine, like an uncoiled spring, like a gentle snake or like a dragon spouting fire. It can be felt like ants crawling in the body. All of these sensations are appropriate. What you can do is stay surrendered and let it do its work. If you feel you are not ready for the experience, you can gently request it to go back to its resting place till such a time when you can trust the process and can stay surrendered. Shakti is a gentle force, as long as we do not resist it. She has her own intelligence that is infinitely wiser than ours.

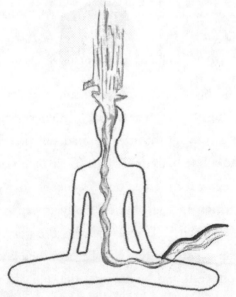

Kundalini rises as a steady stream up the spine.

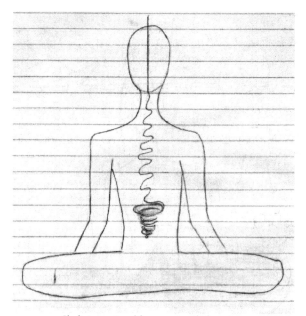

Shakti moving like an uncoiled spring.

Even after I get up from meditation, my body keeps vibrating for almost an hour. What is happening?

This is good because it is an indication that your practice is yielding results. It means that the energy has become active and is moving through the nadis of the subtle body. Because the subtle body meridians (nadis) are not expanded enough to allow for the free flow of energy, they go through a spasm, which in the physical body is experienced as a trembling or jerking. Take a walk on the grass or go hug a tree – the excess energy will be absorbed by the earth through your feet, and by hugging the tree you are passing on the excess energy to it. This will ground you.

According to Master Charles Cannon:

"Kriya in Sanskrit means movement. In a more contemporary understanding, it is meridian spasm. It indicates that the meridians are not able to dilate enough to handle an unrestricted flow of sourceful energetic. Thus, a resistance is created and the spasm in the meridian reflexes into the physical body and is experienced as shaking, twitching and jerking. The old schools acknowledged this process and therefore, placed great emphasis on the integrative or purificatory aspect of the meditator's journey. In the Ashtanga Yoga one had to endure seven years of purificatory techniques before they were allowed to sit for formal meditation."

While meditating, at times my body is still and my head moves in a number eight pattern. The movement is horizontal. What does this symbolise or mean?

Once the shakti is awakened, a process of rebirthing begins. The transition period may not be as beautiful or comfortable because the Kundalini energy is working its way through various stress blocks, emotional issues, and fears that have been built up over the years which would hinder its progress towards the transformational process of the body, mind, and intellect through which it is moving. Your body can go through different postures or breathing patterns. In your experience, the energy is active in the Ajna chakra (centre between the eyebrows) and your head is following the pendulum-like movement of the chakra. This movement or vibration can resemble the shape of the infinity symbol.

When you are following the path of Kundalini Yoga, the energy, when it is active, causes certain kriyas to take place. This is a natural phenomenon. Your body will go through the postures that will facilitate the energy onwards on its path.

A note on the Ajna chakra

When you live life unconsciously, without awareness, it means the Ajna chakra is not active. It is after the awakening of Ajna that you understand the laws of cause and effect.

Ajna chakra is the point where the three main nadis – Ida, Pingla, and Sushumna – merge. Ajna means command, perception, knowledge, and authority. Its colour is purple and indigo. The development of this chakra helps an individual to move from a dualistic mind of right and wrong, good and bad, truth and lie, ugly and beautiful, to an intuitive neutral mind where one views things as they are and moves away from opposites, and one starts accepting situations as they are, without judging them.

Each of the chakras contains stores of karma which may be good or bad, painful or pleasant. The awakening of the chakras will bring to the surface the impressions stored in them, relating to the physical, mental and emotional traumas which one may not be ready or prepared to face. Only those equipped with reason and understanding can cope and that comes only when the Ajna chakra is active.

Working with Ajna helps to focus the mind, bringing forth clarity, peace, inner as well as cosmic knowledge. Ajna is the bridge that links the guru with the disciples. It represents the level at which it is possible for direct mind-to-mind communication between two people.

Ajna is referred to as the third eye, the divine eye, or the eye of intuition that gazes inwards and outwards, thus developing the power of insight and foresight. It also acts as the control centre for the distribution of prana. If the vision of light at the Ajna is well-developed, an aspirant would be able to visualise the flow and movement of prana.

If your energy is dominant in Ajna chakra, a certain peace and serenity arises irrespective of what is transpiring outside of you.

When you give the omkara to indicate the end of meditation, I can't open my eyes. If I force myself out of meditation I feel uncomfortable and because the energy is high, I can't sleep.

First and foremost, never get up abruptly from meditation

no matter if the omkara is given and the others are out of it. You are to stay put till your energy gradually comes into balance. If you get up before the process is complete, you will be fragmented and disoriented. If sleep is not happening, it means the energy is moving towards the head and causing restlessness; use two pillows to support your head so that your body is at a slant and start taking your attention from the top of your head, through each part of your body till you come to your feet. Energy follows thought and as you move down into your body the energy will also follow and will settle down at its resting place, that is, at the base of the spine. You will be asleep as soon as the energy settles.

If you feel overwhelmed and unsure of what to do, then, generally, simple things are safe to follow. You could go for long walks, sit on the grass, or hug a tree. You need to get grounded; this will absorb the excess energy. If you are unsure, fearful and if doubt has set in, it is best to stop all spiritual practice and get on with the mundane chores of life and daily living. This will take away the focus from the energy.

I saw Kali very clearly in my meditation. Is that how gods reveal themselves or is it pure imagination?

You have probably been exposed to the worship of Kali and that has left an impression of the image in your mind, which has been stored as memory. In a relaxed state of meditation, when there is less of body consciousness, certain centres of the brain open up and stored memories or images emerge to the surface. The visions, whether of gods, deities or places, come from memory, from strong visual imprinting of events that take place in our daily life. These are mystical symbols and will relate to the culture and background you come from.

When I sit for meditation many strange sounds come out of my mouth. I am aware of it happening but am unable to control them. What are these sounds?

When you are sitting for meditation in the energy field of the guru, you have the sense of complete acceptance and are secure in the knowledge that in whatever state of being you are, there will be no judgement or labeling. In that relaxed state of being, the process of letting go happens. Sometimes the negative or stressful data and emotions stored in the Mooladhara chakra that we are unable to express from our current state of consciousness, are often expressed through the more basic instincts and so are let out in the form of certain sounds which can be of puppies snapping and growling or the roar of a lion. These sounds come from a time when consciousness existed in primitive or in two emotional states – surviving in comfort and distress.

These are generally termed as kriyas. It is a process of cleansing, and once the clearing has taken place, you get a feeling of good health, happiness, and a zest for life.

A note on the Mooladhara chakra

The Mooladhara chakra is made of the earth element and represents the beginning of life. The fundamental quality of this chakra is innocence and innate wisdom. It represents action without motive and gross personal gain. This chakra controls the survival instinct, inner state of safety and self-confidence. Emotional problems and suffering, loneliness, extreme sensitivity, feeling withdrawn, fear, guilt, lack of trust, passive and aggressive behavior are some of the emotions that block this chakra. If your energy is dormant in the Mooladhara, then food and sleep will be the most dominant factor in your life.

Chakras: The Energy Transformers

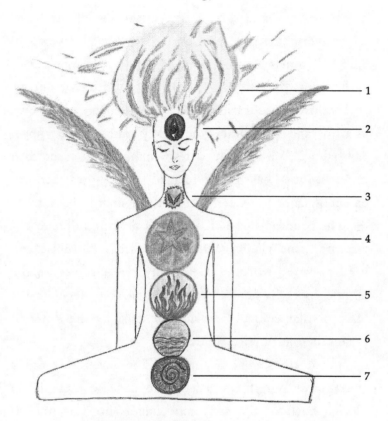

1
2
3
4
5
6
7

Chakras and the Body Temple*
1. Sahasrar chakra (Crown Centre)
2. Ajna chakra (Brow or Third Eye)
3. Vishuddhi chakra (Throat)
4. Anahata chakra (Heart)
5. Manipura chakra (Navel)
6. Swadhisthana chakra (Sacral)
7. Mooladhara chakra (Base)

*This chart showing the location of the seven main chakras in the etheric body is a stylised
version created by the author, and the colours and symbols shown here do not necessarily
correspond to the descriptions in the traditional literature on Kundalini.

According to the seers, the chakras are part of the etheric or subtle body and cannot be seen by the physical eye. The etheric body comprises an extensive network of energy channels. At the points where these channels cross each other, they form a plexus or a centre of energy. In Sanskrit, these intricate channels of energy are known as nadis and the points where they intersect are known as chakras. Where only a few channels intersect each other, minor chakras are formed; where great streams of energy meet and cross, they form major chakras.

The condition of a chakra has a definite influence on the endocrine glands. The chakras are very subtle and high-powered vortices of energy, which receive the cosmic energy. They act as transformers to regulate the force of that energy so it may be used by the different organs in the physical body.

There are six main chakras. The seventh is not a chakra and is termed as a centre because there is no plexus. Each of the six main chakras has its counterpart in the physical body in the form of vital organs (endocrine glands) and vitalises the area around it in the physical body. The health of an organ is dependent on the condition of the associated chakra. The more congested a chakra, the denser the related organ. Congestion of the chakra is related to the physical, mental and emotional baggage an individual body-mind organism carries throughout its evolution. Therefore, the chakras not only control and energise the physical body, but also control and affect the individual's mental and emotional body.

The chakra can change in size, shape and movement according to the situation or emotion. The movement can change from rhythmic to chaotic. It can move like a flipped coin, clockwise or anti-clockwise, up and down like a coin on edge, or left-right, left-right, like the pendulum of a clock. The rhythm changes according to the circumstance, situation, or mood. The rhythm and vibration of the chakra also indicates whether the event is related to a person, place, or thing. It is through their highly developed and sensitive chakras that advanced aspirants can foretell the detail of an event that is to occur, or the identity of a person approaching them.

According to Swami Satyananda Saraswati:

"Awakening of the chakras is a very important event in human evolution. It should not be misunderstood for mysticism or occultism, because with the awakening of the chakras, our consciousness and our mind undergo changes. These changes have significant relevance and relationship with our day-to-day life. The higher qualities of love, compassion, charity, mercy and so on are the expressions of a mind which is influenced by awakened chakras."

It is contemplated that physical energy can be transformed into subtle energy through the actions of the chakras, and also that the physical energy can be converted into mental energy within the physical dimension. As the chakras are activated and awakened, man becomes aware of the higher realms of existence, and also gains the power to enter those realms.

It is essential that the chakras work in synchronicity so that the energy can flow freely. The chakras are vortices of psychic energy and their rhythm of vibration is determined by our feelings, emotions and thought patterns.

During satsang with a master of meditation, there was a constant flow of tears. There was no sadness but the tears would not stop. Please tell me why this happens.

When in the energy field of a master, various emotions like laughter, tears and crying can be manifested as Kundalini energy starts to move through the chakras.

The spontaneous flow of tears is related to the purification of the meridians around the Ajna chakra.

Master Charles Cannon describes in detail the process that is taking place:

"This is associated with the clearing of the ocular meridians related to the third eye vortex. In the

Kundalini traditions, it was referred to as appropriate purification. As the Primary Trinity – physical, mental and emotional – becomes more constant in balance, harmonic coherence (interactive balance) results. With duration in harmonic coherence, the subtle dimensions actualise. The first of these dimensions is termed as the subtle dimension and relates to the third eye vortex. It is your harmonic frequency of vibration that is evolving. The associated meridians dilate, as you multi-dimensionally actualise, and the reflexes can produce tears. The result will be increased constancy in witness consciousness."

As soon as I sit for meditation, there is a constant flow of thoughts. When will the thoughts stop?

The more you dwell on thoughts, the deeper they get fixed in your memory. The only way to stop this from happening is to completely reject the past, and to stop thinking of the future. Do not get involved with the thoughts; remain a witness to them. Just as a plant when neglected wilts and dies, so do thoughts when they are not given attention. This can be accomplished by training yourself to be just a witness, so that you remain in the present.

When all deep-rooted, accumulated impressions are cleared through the practice of meditation, the thoughts will stop. Then what will remain are surface impressions that will flit across the mind as clouds across a sky.

Meditation means being and not doing. What is important is that, as far as possible, you should sit at a fixed time and at fixed place. This is advised because the place you sit at will develop a certain vibration, so that whenever you sit at that place, the already charged area will facilitate the process of meditation. The time is also fixed so that if you are under the guidance of your guru, his energy or vibration starts flowing towards you no matter whether he is physically present or not. Fixed time is stressed because with constant practice you have created a channel which starts to operate at the given time. If you are not present to receive and avail of the energy, it will move on.

You cannot stop the inflow of thoughts. What you can do is to be a witness to them. It is like standing in your balcony and watching the traffic go by. Or, you can bring your attention to the inflow and outflow of your breath. Every time the attention shifts you could come back to your breath. Don't stress yourself trying to focus on it.

The wise tell us that the thoughts that we hold, and the words that we go on repeating, create our life and experience. What we choose to think today will create our tomorrow and so our future. The purpose of meditation is to allow the stored data from the unconscious areas of the mind to surface. This is where we can let go of the old negative data of ill-will, spite, hatred, greed, etc. and experience release. Do not suppress any thoughts that emerge, whether they are of anger, resentment or grief. Allow them to surface and be open to the experience. Be a witness to whatever transpires, because if you suppress any negative emotions, they will release themselves through some means or another like in the form of physical illness, nervous breakdown or aggression in any form.

Master Charles Cannon on Negative Emotions

It is important to keep in mind that true meditation is a clearing process. As we access subtle states of awareness through meditation, the clearing of data will occur from the subconscious and unconscious areas of the mind. This clearing may present itself in many forms, whether through physical, mental or emotional dimensions.

A common experience for those practising meditation is the emergence of negative emotions such as anger, grief, sadness, or loneliness that may arise in conscious experience. What can we do with these thoughts and feelings as the clearing takes place?

Firstly, you need to acknowledge that all experience is valid and so too, is the experience you are having in the moment. Allow and be open to the experience rather than resisting it. What you resist persists, but what you allow begins to flow, allowing clearing to happen. Simply observing emotions as they arise in the moment is the most powerful tool we have to bring balance to any emotional state.

Emotions such as anger are powerful energies, and if suppressed, will find for themselves fragmented and stressful ways of release. As you experience the emotions, avoid the temptation to project them on to another person or thing. Rather, move to the source of the feeling within yourself and allow the emotional energy to express itself in a balanced way.

If observing the emotions is still not enough to deliver stillness in your meditation, you may wish to use the process of affirmation. Use the power of your emotions to strengthen your affirmations and create balance. Statements such as "I am love," "I am the power," and "I am the source of my thoughts and emotions" can transform the negative emotion into a powerful force for creativity and change.

Physical exercise will also greatly assist in the movement and clearing of the emotional energy. Walking, running, dancing or any form of aerobic exercise will support the restoration of balance.

When I sit for meditation, sometimes for days there is a great deal of spinning and movement of energy, whereas there are days when there are only thoughts. Then days follow when there is just boredom. Kindly explain.

The nervous system is very delicate. When the shakti moves, the nervous system goes through a series of changes, therefore, constant activity can be dangerous. And since you are surrendered to the shakti, it knows to what extent your nervous system can be pushed at any given point in time. Once that limit has been reached and the system requires rest, it withdraws to its resting place.

This rest period is also required for the nervous system to assimilate the change that is taking place in order to be prepared for the next level of growth.

When thoughts surface, be a witness and let them pass. What you term as boredom, is a period of rest given to your nervous system. Once that is achieved, the shakti will start its work again. This off and on process will go on till your system is brought to a rhythm, which will facilitate its flow to fulfil the purpose for which it was activated.

Master Charles Cannon on the Mechanics of Balance

For periods of time, your meditations may be powerful and deep, and then, seemingly for no apparent reason, another cycle begins that delivers restlessness, mind chatter, and negative emotions. Wholeness has given way to fragmentation. At such times you may ask yourself what is happening?

As a meditator it is important to be aware of the process that unfolds as you sit for meditation. The mechanics of balance, as they apply to a meditator, are well documented and encompass a three-fold cycle that includes what is known as peak, clearing, and integration.

The practice of meditation builds a foundation of balance. You add momentum to this foundation each time you sit to meditate. Progressively, balance builds power and a transformational process begins. You bring yourself to the peak of your holistic experience and become more than you ever have been. Your meditative practice has pushed the boundaries of your experience and moved you into new territory. This is the peak experience.

Following this peak, a clearing process occurs that includes everything that is incongruent with this more truthful and holistic way of being. The box you were once in has now expanded somewhat, and thus a re-shaping and shifting needs to occur in order to accommodate it. Fragmentation must be jettisoned to make way for wholeness. This clearing can take on a number of forms and is the process that is the basis of the restlessness or upheaval you experience in your meditations.

The cycle then moves into the next phase, which is integration. This is where you become familiar with your new state of being. The new you has now become a more comfortable 'fit', so to speak. The dust has settled and you are ready to repeat the transformational cycle again.

Remind yourself that this cycle is extremely important because it signals that your meditation is working. It provides the feedback that you are evolving and are at the cutting edge of your holistic experience. So, welcome it and embrace the clearing and integration phases of the meditative cycle as appropriate. It's exactly what should be happening.

Sometimes after getting into a meditative state, I am not able to get out of it. Why is that and how can one regulate the process?

It is advised that when an aspirant gets into a regular practice of meditation, he set a time frame for himself. This is necessary because when one gets into deeper states of meditation, the process then completes itself in that time frame and there are lesser chances of getting lost in meditation. I was advised by my guru to set a time frame of half-an-hour to forty-five minutes. If you force yourself out of meditation then there are chances of fragmentation which might lead to a feeling of discomfort and restlessness till the energy settles down.

At times I feel extremely energised. I feel as if my body will just go and hit the ceiling. In meditation, I felt as if I have hit the ceiling and my head has exploded like a volcano and hot, golden lava is flowing out of it from all sides. I saw this happening to me in meditation but my physical body was still.

This is a subtle body experience. When the shakti moves through the subtle body meridians (nadis) the process of purification begins. This may involve the shattering of blocks, mental or emotional, that are blocking its path. Sometimes the force with which the energy moves and breaks the block can give a shock.

The hot, golden lava flowing is the release of the Kundalini energy. So wait and watch what is to unfold for you.

When I went through my experience, I felt as if a bolt of lightning had hit me and my whole body was blown into smithereens. The nervous system has to be very strong to bear this force. (Refer to the section on Kundalini for illustrations.)

Heat seems to rise up my spinal column - from base to top of the head. Sometimes, though, this happens only from the heart level upwards. Why?

Through our breath, we bring prana into our bodies. Prana flows into the body through subtle channels known as nadis. The three most important nadis are Ida on the left of the spine, Pingla on the right, and Sushumna in the centre. Ida and Pingla cross over each other at the chakras whereas Sushumna nadi passes up straight through the centre of each chakra. As we breathe through our nose, we bring prana into our bodies in two distinct currents; positive and negative.

Ida is the channel for mental energy or lunar energy. Pingla is the channel for prana shakti or solar energy. When the breath is flowing more through the right nostril, we say Pingla is active and then one is more energetic and dynamic. When breath is flowing more through the left nostril, we say Ida is active. Ida is the conductor of *manas shakti*, the mental or lunar energy. When this nadi is flowing, then there may be a feeling of tranquility or dreaminess since it is a more passive energy. Sushumna nadi is for spiritual energy. When both nostrils are flowing, we say that Sushumna is active.

Sushumna is the conductor of mahaprana, the spiritual energy of Kundalini. When Sushumna is flowing, it is the most favourable time for any type of sadhana. During this phase a feeling of equanimity and a meditative state can arise spontaneously.

Simply put, with every inhalation through the right nostril, a positive current flows through the Pingla located on the right side of the spine. This is solar energy and it creates heat in the body. When Pingla is flowing, the left side of the brain is active and the right side is quiet.

With every inhalation through the left nostril, a negative current flows through the Ida located on the left side of the spine. This is lunar energy and it cools the body. When Ida is flowing, then the right side of the brain is active and the left side is quiet.

When both Ida and Pingla flow together, i.e. when the right and left hemispheres of the brain function simultaneously, then Sushumna begins to flow. It is said that when Sushumna flows, one just has to close one's eyes and meditation happens.

The heat rising up your spinal column, from the base to the top of your head, indicates that the energy is moving up through Pingla nadi or the solar channel. In other words, it is Pingla that is operative and the breath is flowing through the right nostril. You could balance your energy by consciously doing om-vilom pranayama.

When you feel that your energy is moving up and down from a certain chakra, it means that for that time-being, the particular chakra is acting as the base from which the energy is operating. Since you feel that it is moving up from the Anahata chakra (heart centre) through Vishuddhi and Ajna up to the Sahasrar, it is probably doing so for a very good reason, which only the energy knows or you in your experience would be able to understand as unfolding takes place.

Master Charles Cannon on a Still Mind

There is sometimes confusion that the mind must be completely devoid of thoughts during meditation. This can lead to frustration as the meditator struggles to empty the mind and be totally tranquil. The mind is supposed to think and is part of the multi-dimensional experience of being human. An alternative perspective to denying the mind is to embrace it as part of meditative experience.

Rather than identifying with the thinking, become the detached witness to your experience and allow the thoughts to be appropriate. Witness consciousness is the detached observation of what is happening in the moment. If thinking is happening allow it to be so.

An analogy often used in relation to thinking during meditation is that of clouds floating by in the sky.

The clouds representing as thoughts, come and go, but the sky always remains clear and blue behind the clouds. Identify with the blue sky rather than the clouds.

By bringing awareness to the mind and allowing the thoughts to be as they are, the mind will become more balanced. With balance it will be easier to witness the thinking as just one dimension of a multi-dimensional state of being. Eventually the thoughts will become an entertainment rather than something to be avoided in meditation.

I was sitting for meditation with my back resting against a wall in a Shiva temple. When the time came to get up, I realised that I could not move. Is there any explanation for something like this?

This experience can occur in relation to a person, place or thing that is highly charged with energy. When a receptive aspirant enters this highly charged magnetic field, he can get into a 'locked in' posture. Temples, caves, churches, or any such place where worship and chanting are regular features, can elicit this kind of a response from an aspirant as a kind of fusion between the two energies takes place. The release will take place when the equilibrium between the aspirant's energy and the magnetic field happens. Just stay relaxed and be a witness of your experience. Don't force yourself to get up.

'Locked in' means when you get rooted to a spot. Your senses stop functioning and every part of your body, mind, and intellect get fixed. It is like the 'statue' game children play.

I remember when I went through this experience. I had gone to the Mahalaxmi temple one early morning to get a photograph I had of Durga Ma blessed. The morning's first puja was performed on the photograph. I brought it home and reverentially placed it in my altar. Next morning, when I lit the lamp, opened the altar door, and sat for meditation, a strong gust of energy hit me like a tornado and I was 'locked' in the posture in which I was sitting. Though I was aware of all that was going around me, I could not move. My senses and limbs were fixed. The only thing that I could do was to stay rooted till such a time when the lock released itself.

When you are on a spiritual journey, you are not in control, there are higher forces that take charge and whatever is required for your spiritual growth will be implemented.

During meditation, I saw myself going up and down coloured tiles as if I am climbing up and down a staircase. The colours are red, blue, orange, yellow, green, and pink. Could you please explain this?

During meditation you are moving in the region of the

unknown, so what you see, you interpret according to your understanding and relevant visual impact the experience conveys.

What you were visualising during meditation is the movement of Kundalini up and down the spinal column, and in the process, it illuminated the colours of the chakras it was moving through. You perceived the vertebrae in the spinal column as a stairway of tiles.

The two figures below symbolically represent the spine as visualised by an aspirant (on the left) and as visualised by myself (on the right).

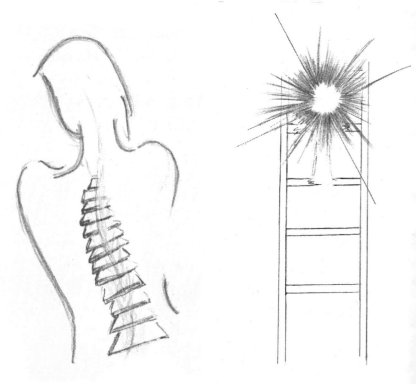

I had a similar experience, during the period of my spiritual growth, wherein I visualised the spine as a ladder with consciousness moving up the ladder. When it reached the top of the ladder, the last two rungs snapped with a loud, splintering sound. My consciousness had broken a barrier leading to another level of awareness.

While meditating I sometimes hear sounds that no one else hears. They are sounds of popping, snapping or an explosion set off. What does this mean?

These sounds emanate from the subtle body. When there is a block in the path of Kundalini, then the nearby chakra begins to move. The chakra's movement gets accelerated. Because of this movement, a particular energy is created, which breaks the block. This process goes on at different levels. The blocks are the result of the negative data one has collected over lifetimes and is stored in the form of congealed energy at different levels of one's mental and emotional bodies. Depending on how congealed or dense the energy is in a particular area lying as a block on the path of Kundalini, the relevant pressure will be applied for Kundalini to move on. It is just like when creating a tunnel, the engineer either digs, drills or blasts the rock to clear the path. The activity happening in the subtle body meridians is experienced in the physical as a sudden jerk or shock, accompanied by the relevant sound, depending on the intensity of the breakthrough. With the removal of the blocks some of our karmas are wiped out. This I see as a gift of the Kundalini; because the blocks, which might have taken years to dissolve or sometimes even a lifetime, are removed in a moment and we do not have to live through them or work them out physically in the form of illness.

Are your meditations guided ones?

The guiding force is the guru-field. The guru awakens the shakti and then the shakti itself becomes the master, guiding the aspirant from within or without.

How can I reach a state of stillness in meditation?

You cannot do anything to reach a state of stillness in meditation. It has to happen. It depends on your physical, mental and emotional state. If the three bodies are in balance and you are totally relaxed, it will be quite easy to withdraw attention from your body. Once that happens, you will slip into the state of stillness.

I am an editor by profession and invariably get material related to the scriptures. Over the past two days when I sit for meditation, I have been experiencing a vibrant circle of light on the wall behind me. What does this indicate?

When you are regular in your practice of meditation, a purification of the body at the physical and subtle body levels takes place and this gets reflected in your aura.

The circle of light that you are seeing behind your head when you are meditating is reflecting the state of your mind.

This happens to anyone who is engaged in any form of concentrated mental activity, whether a scientist, poet or painter. The quality of the light will depend upon the nature of the focus.

For further clarification, you could refer to the illustration on p. 163 of *Kundalini Awakening*.

How do I ascertain if these experiences of sound, lights etc. are real?

Any experience in meditation is a subtle body experience and is real. A true practitioner of meditation actually sees real lights and hears real sounds. These will keep manifesting until one goes beyond them. When one experiences them directly, there is never any doubt. That is why the masters do not encourage any reading on the subject until an aspirant has not gone through his experience. The way to distinguish between an aspirant who is projecting the experience and an aspirant who is going through the experience, is to observe them. The one who has had the experience will be light-hearted, full of joy, and at peace. In such a person, the process of transformation has begun.

Master Charles Cannon on Thoughts

All thoughts are released as soon as you create them. Bring a thought into manifestation within the mind and you simultaneously manifest it through the universe. As in the microcosm, so in the macrocosm. This is the law of creation. Just as you store thoughts as beliefs in the unconscious, so also those thoughts/ beliefs are stored in the collective unconscious. There is no eraser as in a little piece of rubber that makes it all disappear. The only way to erase is through dissolution and this is accomplished through balance. When two polarities balance each other in the unconscious, they dissolve each other. Then through balance awareness expands.

During meditation, pain and sorrow from many lifetimes seems to accumulate in my legs and then slowly leaks out of the toes. The legs feel thick and clogged as if circulation of blood has stopped. I then hear some gentle cracking sounds, like the snapping of fingers. With the completion of this process, the clogged energy flows out through the toes and my legs feel much better. I rub them down after the meditation and they feel normal.

The sequence of your experience indicates that a process of cleansing and purification is going on in the Mooladhara chakra. This chakra is the storehouse of all the guilt, every complex and agony. It is very important to awaken this chakra and get out of it. The activation of this chakra has brought the latent pain and trauma stored in the cell memory of your body to the surface, and it is being pushed downwards and out. The snapping sound in the subtle body is of the blocks breaking and releasing the clogged energy. Once the blocks are dissolved completely, you will feel a release and a spring in your step.

In meditation, I sometimes get the feeling of wings flapping gently in my head. What does this mean?

In my experience, I have usually visualised the wings at the level of the Ajna chakra and the Anahata chakra. These are vibrations of the chakras, which take on the shape of wings.

C.W. Leadbeater in his book *The Chakras* tells us that, "the wings typify the power of conscious flight through higher planes." The wing-like vibrations of the heart chakra would mean that an aspirant is moving towards compassion, and giving of unconditional love. One can understand why we usually see paintings of angels having wings.

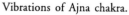

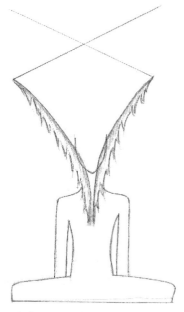

Vibrations of Ajna chakra.   Vibrations of Anahata chakra.

During a group meditation, a shape like a dish antenna appeared above my head and kept moving in different directions as if it were collecting information. What does this mean?

Scriptures have depicted Kundalini coded in symbology. Now that the consciousness has evolved, the time has come to decode those symbols and to arrive at the hidden meaning.

You will see in the illustration given below the flowering of the Sahasrar (crown) centre, extending outward in all directions and bringing forth expanded awareness. This is said to be the centre of higher consciousness.

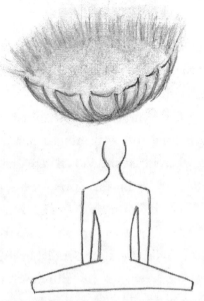

The expanded vibrations of the Sahasrar:
the thousand-petalled lotus.

When the progressive ascension of Kundalini through the chakras culminates at the Sahasrar, then the vibrations of this centre act and take the shape of a radar or as symbolically expressed, a 'thousand-petalled lotus'. All knowledge gained henceforth would be self-gained and not necessarily bookish knowledge.

I have heard some people narrate experiences of Kundalini even though they do not follow any Kundalini technique or have a guru. How is this possible?

These days there are various workshops being conducted on yoga, pranayama, chakras and mass Kundalini awakening etc. These activities can produce a premature awakening and if the teacher is not equipped to guide the awakened energy it can prove to be harmful at the physical, mental and emotional level.

Normally with the awakening of Kundalini, a guru is essential. In rare cases, the awakening happens due to the past samskaras wherein an individual has practised some form of sadhana and at an appropriate time in this life, the symptoms of Kundalini manifest to lead the individual to his next level of growth. In this situation, if the individual can surrender, then the Kundalini itself becomes the guru. However, even in this situation, the person, instead of getting confused and groping in the dark, will have to seek the mentorship of a living guru who can give him guidance.

Why do bad experiences appear to get manifested when I pursue meditation seriously?

This is a very serious and valid question. Meditation should improve the quality of one's life and not impair it. Yet the experience is near universal – serious meditation makes things worse, before they get better. The simple answer is that meditation speeds up the process of evolution; issues and problems that may never have surfaced in an ordinary life spring to the surface and require to be dealt with attentively.

If one is following a form of meditation which is linked with Kundalini, then catharsis is bound to happen. When the Kundalini starts to move and meets with resistance, then the nearby chakra becomes active. The chakra begins to move at a certain speed and because of this movement, intense energy is created which breaks the block. With the breaking of the block, stored data (life experiences related to that chakra) is released which then surfaces during meditation.

Chakras are not just vibrating nodes of energy. They are mechanisms for collecting and processing karma. Meditation causes the chakras to become more active, and karma is shaken loose. In serious meditation, there will always be stages where karmic impediments arise. Unless they are dealt with, one cannot progress. Hence, these sudden surges of unpleasant incidents occur. Far from being disheartened, such episodes should be encouraging because they are proof that you are doing something right.

The goal of serious meditation is not to become more productive at work or dispel insomnia. It is to attain enlightenment and liberation. That is not possible without flushing out all the negative karma.

GENERAL QUESTIONS

You have had extraordinary experiences and I have read your record of all you went through. Can you share with us how that has actually changed your perspective in life?

It is not that the situations in life change. It is our perspective that changes. The situation stays the same, but the response to it is what changes. When Kundalini is awakened, our body and consciousness change. It is not an overnight transformation, but a process of gradual change that occurs by being in the energy field of the guru and through the interaction that occurs because of it.

This also means that one is always aware of the messages coming through the guru, whether directly or indirectly. Awareness will lead to understanding and understanding will lead to acceptance. When you can accept yourself, all your limitations, insecurities and your fears will fade away to be replaced with abundance, wisdom and hope. If the teaching is practised with respect and reverence, it will change your life. You will experience freedom from past relationships and will move towards an expanded state of consciousness.

Constant awareness and practise has helped me to live the teaching. Each one of us will respond and imbibe the teaching according to our psyche and need.

I know you live with your children and go about your daily duties like before, but yet you have a heightened sense of awareness that we don't. Can you tell us something about that?

To live in constant awareness is not to avoid situations in life or even in myself, but to learn to accept them and know their nature. This would require a state of mind that is continuously observant of the nature of events; to develop the ability to see the reality behind situations other than what appears to be, and to look at things in their positive as well as negative aspect.

I have learnt not to jump to conclusions but to look at things from the other's perspective. We have all come with our own scripts and the way which the drama of our life should unfold. Unfortunately very few scripts match. So, the good player is the one who has the awareness to pick up the cue that the other's dialogue offers and give an appropriate response. This requires one to be 'present' in the moment and always alert. I have learnt not to judge, complain or blame, and to accept everything as is.

I remember an instance from a dialogue between Swami Shivom Tirth and his disciple. The disciple asked Swamiji that suppose he stumbled on a stone, would it mean that he was lacking in awareness. Swamiji said, "very definitely so."

The change is not only experienced in my life. I can see it reflected in my children's lives also. They are living their life in awareness. The sages have said that when one person in a family gets on the spiritual path – the grace is experienced by seven generations. I can well believe that, for when a change in consciousness occurs in one person in a family, his/her language, action and behaviour would invite a similar response.

A Zen master was asked how his life changed when he became enlightened. He replied, "Well, before enlightenment, I would carry water and chop wood. After enlightenment, I carry water, and chop wood."

Even after he became enlightened, he still went about his day doing whatever he did before, but since he was now enlightened, he was able to chop wood and carry water without distraction.

What the proverb "Chop wood, carry water" means is that life will be what it was before. Enlightenment makes no difference, life continues the way it always was.

How do you explain these experiences of light and Kundalini awakening that you have experienced? Is the light you see the same as anyone else having a similar experience? Or is everyone's experience different? In which case, which is the reality? Yours or theirs?

My experience has come through the grace of the guru. This light is not the light of the light bulb. It is a light that the Ajna chakra or the third eye throws into the region of the unconscious. This vision enables one to see what is not visible to the physical eye. Everyone will go through their own experience according to their culture, nature, and conditioning, and they create their own reality based on a foundation of balance or imbalance they maintain in their mind.

I read in Gopi Krishna's book 'A Path to Higher Consciousness' that these images of light, or even other people's experiences of seeing Krishna or Jesus etc. are only a figment of the mind. The mind translates such experiences into a language that can easily be understood by the person having that experience. For example, Mira Bai saw Krishna and not Jesus, while St. Therese saw Jesus and not Shiva. What do you say about that?

What is a figment of the mind? What does one perceive the mind to be? Where do all these images come from? They come from inner experiences, from strong visual imprinting.

I perceive the mind to be the data bank of the master computer or the akashik records of a particular body, mind, and intellect. When the light of consciousness is thrown on the subtler dimensions of the mind, it will throw up the data that is stored in the unconscious.

It may relate to your present cultural data or when your consciousness was a part of another culture in an earlier lifetime. Nothing is a figment of the imagination.

Our imagination will only project what we have experienced. People with no access to books or to India see Maha Avatar Babaji. Master Charles Cannon saw Swami Muktananda in his vision before he began formal sadhana and before coming to India. So it is not as if these things are limited to culture and knowledge. One of Swami Yogananda's American disciples saw Swami Vivekananda in a vision before meeting either of them in life. So Meera seeing Lord Krishna and others seeing Jesus is probably a choice based on emotions and spiritual longings as well as the many lives in which the soul was inclined in a particular direction.

As a householder how do I balance my spiritual life with my daily life?

As a householder you can go about daily living in full awareness i.e. whatever task you are doing, give it your full attention and that becomes your daily meditation.

What do the terms 'detachment' and 'involvement' mean?

Detachment represents a state of mind that is constantly observant of the nature of events and that remains unaffected by them. Once you realise that you can be a witness to the events taking place in your life, your awareness will expand and you will be able to see the reality behind situations. Detachment implies that no matter what is going on in your mind, no matter what you are thinking, rather than identifying with the thinking, you become the detached witness to what is transpiring in the moment. If thinking is happening, allow it to be so. The task is to learn to detach from petty ideas and feelings. In other words, detachment means going beyond delusion and opposites.

Verse 213 of the Dhammapada says, "Emotional ties bring only sadness and fear. Avoid attachment in emotion and you avoid sadness and fear." Once we are attracted to something, then our ego and the possessive quality of our nature is manifested. Detachment on the other hand, involves a state of mind in which you use your discretion and act accordingly. It is not a game of action and reaction but of stimulus and response.

'Involvement' means getting involved with a thought or situation and creating a drama out of it by getting into the why, how and what of it by oscillating between the past and the future, both of which do not exist. The past is dead and gone and the future is yet to be. Do not confuse involvement with attachment. Attachment creates illusions and desires. If a desire is unfulfilled, then what arises is anger. One thing leads to another, and anger leads to confusion. Once that happens one fails to use one's reason. This downward slide stems from a single unfulfilled desire.

I have heard several masters tell us that on our journey to finding the Truth, we must keep our focus and clarity on the final objective and not get distracted by events and changes that come to us in the process. In other words, that if we get too involved with the siddhis or our experiences of light or channeling, we could live in the wonder of exploring rather than aiming for the Truth. What do you think?

My guru also emphasised the same and saw to it that I went through each and every experience without getting attached to it. I feel that the guru shows you the way and the individual psyche takes its own direction. For myself, I have chosen the path of 'just being', i.e. allowing life to work through me for whatever purpose. If any manifestation has to happen it will happen. There is no 'will' involved. In the path of siddhis one gets into the 'doing' mode and unless one is a highly evolved soul, a 'siddha', who can see into the past, present, and future of the person concerned, this can do more harm than good. One is interfering with the individual's karma as well as one's own karma. Siddhis are for the siddhas. My guru's advice to me was that if I wanted to be of help to anyone, I should make an 'intention' and leave it at that. The Source will take care of it.

Is it necessary to have a guru? It is said that 'when the disciple is ready the guru will appear'. I visit different masters, how will I know which one is my guru?

Yes, when you are ready your guru will appear. When the question, "is this my guru?" does not arise, when there is total acceptance and your ego drops, then you have found your guru. There will be signs for you to pick up, if you are in awareness. His magnetic field will draw you in.

I had my awakening in the energy field of my guru. I don't think it could have happened otherwise and even if it happened through grace, I would have had no road map for guidance. An aspirant enters an unknown zone and if there is no one to guide him, he can get lost and then it may not be easy to find his way back.

Swami Satyananda Saraswati says:

"Without a guru, you can practise any form of yoga, but not Kundalini... So if you want to follow the path of Kundalini Yoga, it is absolutely essential to have a guru with whom you feel intimate... The relationship between guru and disciple is the most intimate of relationships; it is neither religious nor a legal relationship. Guru and disciple live like an object and its shadow."

Master Charles Cannon on the relationship between guru and disciple:

"Alone there is no happiness. Therefore, the Pure Consciousness assumes the form of guru and disciple."

– Jnaneshwar

Revealed in the simple verse above, is a mystical understanding of the master-disciple relationship that gives deep insight into its origin. What it points towards is an entirely different paradigm for relationship that begins from a platform of fullness and extends itself on the love-based principle of happiness. As the verse states, it is Pure Consciousness itself that motivates the guru-disciple relationship, rather than the sense of need or lack.

The master is already full and it is the disciple's own developing awareness resonating with this fullness that pulls him or her into the master's orbit. It is not a fear-based dependency, but a rather natural attraction to the unfolding bliss one feels in the energetic source field of the master that underlies the relationship. Thus, the common shortcomings of ordinary relationships are not found in the master-disciple relationship.

The guru is the greatest benefactor and ally of the disciple. Wisely and compassionately, the guru assists in many ways, both seen and unseen. This is not to say that the guru needs to be aware of all the details in every situation. Sourceful awareness is like a cosmic computer... it can take into account all the complexities without having to address them one by one.

As a pure reflector of Sourceful awareness, everything that comes into the guru's sphere is handled at the Source itself. Thus, obstacles and limitations to the unfolding of wholeness and unity-consciousness in the disciple's journey are spontaneously dissolved. But, if the disciple is moving unconsciously in a direction that is sure to lead to confusion and misery, an obstacle is created at that juncture to prevent the disciple's distraction. In this way, the disciple is compelled to turn in a different, and more conscious, direction.

When the guru says "Yes" or "No", it is in the best interest of the disciple to fully embrace the directive. It is easy to respond to the master's encouragement to what we have already decided, but to relinquish one's attachment at the master's 'behest' directly or indirectly is much more difficult. Thus, it can be understood that whether the master says "Yes" or "No", it is always in the best interest of the disciple to fully embrace the directive.

How does the guru's grace occur?

Through the disciple's reverence, devotion, love, and surrender to the guru.

What is meant by a positive mind?

There is a negative aspect and a positive aspect to the mind. I remember my grandmother admonishing my father when he expressed lack of finances or was negative in his conversation. She would keep telling him "shubh, shubh bolo" – "utter positive words." Our mother would tell us the same thing. But I realised the importance and necessity of it only when I came in contact with my guru.

Think of your mind as a house that has been neglected for a long time. There is a whole lot of junk that has been stored, along with what has also been inherited. The only way to get rid of it is by bringing in new material that will give one comfort and joy.

Similarly, our mind hoards outdated notions or inherited beliefs that are no longer required and should be thoroughly cleared out to make place for positive and relevant data relating to the new consciousness that is emerging. All negative values should be discarded and replenished with positive values of love, beauty and truth.

A positive mind does not merely abstain from jealousy, but is happy in the prosperity of others. It does not merely refrain from hating, but it loves. It does not just tolerate, but it forgives. It does not stop telling lies but it, more often than not, speaks the truth. It does not only stop being greedy, but becomes more giving. Whenever you observe yourself thinking negatively, consciously direct your thinking into the positive through the use of affirmations. Constant vigilance will lead to transformation.

Master Charles Cannon on Energy and Matter

The negative is the contractive polarity that enables energy to become matter. Thus, there would be no human experience possible without its dominance in universal manifestation. In conscious living, since the negative is always dominant, we must be vigilant to consistently emphasise the positive polarity in order to build and maintain the relative balance through which there is witness consciousness. This is directed thinking and feeling. Whenever we notice the mind automatically thinking its dominant negative data, we consciously direct our thinking into the positive through the use of affirmations. Also, we direct our emotions and feelings the same way. We flow positive energy. You must go slow enough to ensure that you are experiencing what you are affirming. In this way, the physical, mental and emotional dimensions will come into balance and subtler dimensional witness consciousness will appear.

What is the nature of the mind?

The nature of the mind is to follow our attention. If our attention focuses on beautiful scenery, the mind will go there. If our attention is somewhere within us, the mind will go there. If our attention is focused on a thought, the mind will take on the form of that thought. If one is feeling sad, the mind will take on sadness. The mind does not have a faculty of its own, it goes in the direction given by the senses.

Should one talk about one's experiences to friends and family?

If your friends and family are tuned into the spiritual life, they will value whatever you share with them. If not, then you can invite ridicule, disbelief, and a question mark on your sanity. It is best to talk to your guru or to others who are going through their awakening. Every experience has a meaning and if you do not understand it or take it just as a happening, you will have lost an opportunity to progress on the path. So, your experience is precious – value it.

I am a cranio-sacral practitioner. When I started a session with a client, neither of us had any intention of awakening Kundalini but it seemed to have awakened on its own. It produced some mild undulations in the body and made my patient arch her back and re-adjust her body position a few times. All this was also accompanied by deep, loud breathing that seemed very cleansing in nature. Towards the end, my client ended up in a very energised and awake, yet grounded, state. She was told in the Bihar School of Yoga that Kundalini awakening should happen only under the supervision of a guru, and it's very dangerous if the energy gets stuck around the Manipura chakra. Is that true?

Yes, it's true. Once the Kundalini awakens, it needs to be guided by someone who understands the energy and can give it direction. It is dangerous if it moves into a chakra if the issues related to that chakra have not been resolved, because the nature of the energy is to enhance the prevalent qualities of that chakra to the optimum. Awakening of Kundalini requires constant monitoring and counseling by the teacher or guru under whose guidance she is.

If a person's physical, mental and emotional bodies are in balance, the process can be smooth and fulfilling.

On the third cranio-sacral session, her body began exhibiting very large undulations with the back and neck arching, and the chest making circular movements etc. These undulations continued in the car on the way back from the session, and have been going on now for a couple of months. They don't disrupt her daily schedule and she can easily will these movements whenever she wants. It's definitely not her that's making them, rather, they seem to be controlled by some inner force. After a month, she found that by simply putting her hands on a particular part of the body, she could produce the undulating movement in that spot. She also became inspired to put her hands on other people, including her husband and children.

The above statement is contradictory. She says that 'the movements come back whenever she wants'. And then she says it is not her that is making them.

The question of activating the energy at will does not arise. The energy movement may happen; it cannot be ordered. She has to surrender to the energy and then flow with the guidance. When she is putting her hands on a particular part of her body, she is focusing and activating that chakra and her body begins to move with the rhythm of the chakra's vibration. For example, if you observe the movement of a pendulum when you are dangling it from a chain, you will see that it moves sideways, up and down, backward and forward, clockwise or anti-clockwise. In the same manner, a chakra also moves in a certain rhythm and, if a person is sensitive, he may reflect the movement through the physical body.

You may exercise your will in other areas of your life but if you are going through the process of Kundalini, it is best to surrender to the energy, otherwise you can do harm to your nervous system.

If your patient is inspired to put her hands on other people, it is probably for some purpose. She should find out for herself how this action helps the people concerned.

Note: *When I am sitting for meditation with my group, I do not tell the energy that radiates from me what to do. It just moves out and, its own wisdom directs itself to take whatever form is needed for the recipients. Since I am not directing it, I do not know what form it takes for them. It's the unconscious of the person who receives it, and his own divine guidance decides how that energy works. After the meditation, people sometimes share their experience of how it worked for them. For instance, if someone came in with a headache, the headache gets cleared. If someone is feverish, she feels energetic. Bodies take on different postures. I actually wouldn't know how people are affected unless they tell me. When one surrenders to the Kundalini energy, it is left to the energy to take whatever form it decides.*

Do you still have visual experiences?

No. The visual experiences ended when the impressions stored in the memory relating to a particular knowledge were exhausted. If any samskaras of this type surface in the future, then I might have the related visual experience again.

I don't know if this has anything to do with the pulsing light circle above my shoulders, but my body has begun exuding a very peculiar aroma that gets into all my clothes and has marinated my skin. Actually, it's very pleasant and people think I am wearing some kind of exotic perfume. What is truly strange is that today, even my urine and stool had the same odour! I am not getting carried away by the phenomena trap, but it is unusual and not to acknowledge it is also untruthful. It smells like some kind of agarbatti.

There is no reason why you should not acknowledge your own experience. Move ahead with understanding and acceptance and, most importantly, with an attitude of gratitude. It is said that the guru field awakens the shakti, and then the shakti leads you on the path of perfection.

All phenomena are indicators that bring to your awareness the process of purification that is going on in your body. The sense of smell is associated with the earth element of the Mooladhara chakra. All psychic smells manifest here. In the case of your experience, the circle of light behind your head and the fragrance is manifesting because your Ajna chakra, which means 'command' or 'the monitoring centre', is focused on the Mooladhara chakra.

The Mooladhara chakra, besides being the store house of guilt and all pain and trauma, is also the seat of Annamaya Kosha that is connected with the absorption of food and elimination, therefore, the reason for the fragrance emanating through the stool and urine. The purification of this chakra would mean good health and a more cheerful disposition.

For understanding this further, you could look at p. 163 of *Kundalini Awakening*. Since my experience of the chakras is in the form of their element, you will see that the earth element of Mooladhara chakra has moved up to the Ajna chakra and the resultant creativity blooms in the form of a green plant.

I had gone to an ashram and during meditation on the banks of the Ganga, I had a past-life experience. In this experience, I saw myself as a soldier on a battlefield, which reminded me of the Mahabharat war. I saw myself fallen on the ground and my limbs being crushed under the wheels of a chariot. When I came out of the meditation, I was still carrying the trauma and the pain in my limbs and had a swelling in my joints. Can you please explain this?

It is observed that when people go through a course of past-life regression or hypnosis, they invariably drop an ailment or a fear (if they have any) once they become aware that their psyche is still carrying a memory of a past life or a childhood experience that no longer exists. In meditation, you also go through the same process, i.e. you become the witness of the scene that is being projected. However, in your case the process was reversed. Instead of just being a detached observer of the experience, your psyche got emotionally identified with the pain and brought it back with you.

If you resonate with this understanding, you can drop the pain. Otherwise, as the memory of the experience fades, the pain you have brought back will also fade and clear out in due course.

What are kriyas, and what is their purpose?

When an aspirant resonates with the spiritual practice, then the energy that is released needs to clear its path so it can move smoothly. With this movement, a purification of the chakras and the Panch Koshas begins with the result that the body goes through involuntary kriyas in the form of yogic postures, emitting different sounds, or singing, shedding tears, and dancing. All the accumulated impressions of lifetimes are thus released and cleared out. Once the purification has been completed, the kriyas will stop.

If I follow some course designed to help me evolve spiritually, how would I know whether I am moving in the right direction?

Please understand that transformation does not happen overnight. If you are diligent in your practice and follow the teaching in a prescribed manner, you are sure to experience results.

Paramahansa Yogananda has underlined the eight aspects of God. If you can observe yourself and identify which of the aspects you are imbibing through your sadhana, you will be able to know whether you are progressing in your practice and at what pace.

"God is infinite and beyond logic but He has eight aspects which can be experienced," says Paramahansa Yogananda. These are:

1. Light – Prakasham
2. Sound – Nadam
3. Peace – Shanti
4. Calmness or stability – Sthiratham/Sthiram
5. Love – Premam
6. Joy – Anandam
7. Wisdom – Gyanam
8. Power – Shakti

I have been practising a self-development course for a number of years. I have had experiences that have helped me to be the balanced person I am today. I would like to teach the same course so that it can help others who want to be helped. My guru is no longer in his body. Can I teach the course?

It depends on the parampara or tradition of the course you are practising. Did your guru formally assign people to teach the course? If there is an assigned teacher, then you could take his advice. In the yogic parampara, it is very clear that you do not teach unless your guru tells you to. Along with intellectual knowledge, and the experiential knowledge of Kundalini movement, teaching requires an emptying of the ego, dropping off the false pride of doership, and performing all dutiful actions with a sense of surrender. Further, one must have the ability to be a clear channel or a hollow bamboo, so that the energy of the guru-field can flow through you.

However, if pride sets in, the energy flow will stop. If you meet the above requirements, the answer will come in your meditation.

What is a psychic attack? How does a person defend against a pre-planned malicious attack without resorting to gems, pujas, and talismans?

Psychic attacks are thought forms of other people. They can be random thought forms not necessarily directed at you, but you might be in their way. For example, if you are in a train, a person may casually be looking at you while he is processing some negative thoughts. There is no intention on that person's part but you are in the path of the thought and, because of your vulnerability, you catch the thought that may result in a depression, bad stomach or some sort of reaction that would clear out in due course. Invariably, we naturally discard most thought-forms that are sent our way. Usually, the person sending the thought has no idea that they can cause pain to someone who is sensitive and intuitive. If a family member is the one directing the negative thought at you, the aura does not protect you since you are more open and vulnerable to that person's familiar thought forms.

There maybe psychic attacks by wayward spirits and people who are into certain negative practices. These attacks will only take effect if an individual is weak-minded, fearful, or comes from certain belief systems. The real test is how a person deals with life-challenging situations in the physical realm. If an individual has a strong energy field, meaning he is by nature confident, fearless, and has an optimistic attitude to life, the attacks will be deflected, or the inherent energy lying within will naturally move up to dispel the attack.

Any psychic attack will have an effect if you leave yourself open to it and accept it. Such a person would be generally fearful, easily dominated by people and circumstances with an attitude of helplessness and pessimism. If, however, you have unconsciously accepted it and you become aware of it before it moves in through your aura, you can just drop it, brush the thought off or have a salt-water bath to wash it off. Given below are four illustrations depicting my experience of a psychic attack.

In meditation, one is usually open. In the above figures, you see that the negative thought first circles the body. Then, it builds up as a threatening cloud over the head, ready to engulf the whole being. The mechanism (Kundalini shakti) of the body becomes active and like a

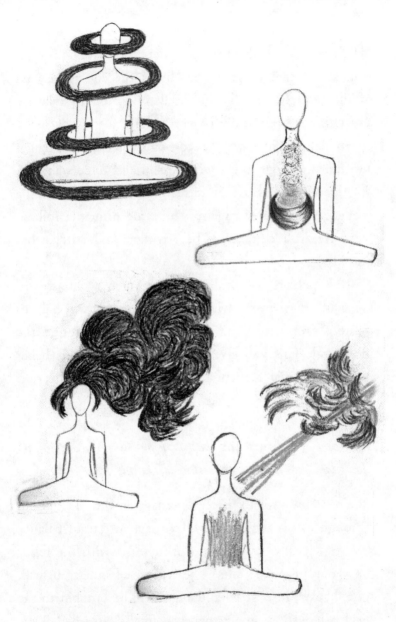

Four illustrations depicting my experience of a psychic attack.

lion roaring, it moves up and in its passage becomes light that dispels the negative energy or psychic attack. This shows that if we do not block the energy because of the fear that arises, our body is geared to take on any challenge physically or psychically.

In daily living, we are constantly facing challenges and move through them with reason and understanding. We do not turn back or retreat. This would mean the challenge will surface again. The same principle follows when we are meditating – be a witness and watch what unfolds.

If a person is timid by nature, gems, pujas, and talismans, if energised with relevant mantras, will help to create a protective vibration or energy field around the individual. This will give him confidence and his belief in the particular gem, mantra or puja will do the rest. It is an individual's choice.

Time and again one hears that happiness is a 'state of mind'. How does one achieve that state of mind?

One of the ways is to practise pranayama and meditation. Through this practice you will achieve a state of balance and your level of awareness will increase, with the result that your negative traits – jealousy, selfishness, ill-will, spite, hatred, lust, greed and anger will be brought to the surface, looked at, understood and finally discarded. They will be substituted with the qualities of love, peace, equanimity, selflessness, and unconditional love for all. With this happening, you will observe that you are much happier and are also spreading happiness around you because the realisation dawns that all is your projection and, consequently, there is no expectation, complaint or blame. The wrong values drop off by themselves, and the right, permanent values are adopted. With this transformation, you achieve the 'state of mind' in which you do not require external stimulants to make you happy. Happiness arises from within and is self-dependent.

How should a person in sadhana react to personal attacks and troubles, especially when they seem unmerited?

The answer is simple: do not react, but respond.

Reaction is an un-thought, knee-jerk, immediate answer to a situation which one takes as a personal attack. Sometimes, one does not even wait for the communication to get completed, and pre-empting it leaves a person confused, hurt or offended. On the other hand, when one makes a studied, intelligent response, it means that the person has given the situation full attention and has, with awareness, responded to it. This lends a completely different perspective to the situation. When you respond, it means you are trying to understand where the other person is coming from, and not from where you think he is coming from. You have detached your personal self from the situation and, from the perspective of an impartial observer, your response will determine the consequences and the results which will most definitely be more objective.

You will say that's easier said than done. Remember, you cannot choose the situations; they arise unbidden, but you can choose how you will respond to them, and in that choice lies your freedom. Instead of complaining about the cards you have been dealt with, you can concentrate on playing them well. It requires a great deal of practise, and you will have to put in that effort so that, from going through life unconsciously which is what a 'reaction' is, you move into conscious living. This is the only way to remove oneself from the action-reaction consequence loop that is Karma.

Another way of understanding this is that it is important to remember that whatever happens to us is a consequence of our *Prarabdha* karma that has already begun to manifest itself. Prarabdha implies the accumulation of instances in our memory as we meet the challenges that life brings forth. These challenges leave their impression on the chitta or consciousness. In order to work out ones prarabdha, one has to work at self-change. This process is unstoppable, although we can mitigate its severity. What is happening to us is an external manifestation of an internal imperative. The abuse or unpleasant experiences we endure, seemingly without merit, are all caused by the Prarabdha squaring karmic accounts. A worldly person sees all incidents and persons in the world as cause of all that occurs in his life.

The more you react, the deeper the grooves of conditioning form in the mind, and it becomes all the more certain that such situations will continue to manifest themselves. The deeper an unpleasant experience sinks into the chitta or mind-stuff, the more likely it is to keep manifesting again and again, and not just in this lifetime! The samskaras or karmic tendencies become hardwired and you find yourself living the same situations again and again.

"We attract what we are," is a blunt, psychological (and yogic) truth. Be happy, and be in the moment, for this will burn off old karma, because you will no longer be oscillating between the past and the future and the negative aspects related to it.

How does one get out of repetitive patterns of behaviour and interaction which we know are futile and self-destructive?

"Habit," said Mark Twain, "is not second nature. It is ten times nature." From a yogic perspective, a habit is condensed energy vibrating in a static mode. In theory, even one day of concentrated effort should clear it. Paramahansa Yogananda used to say that the habits of years could be renounced in an instant, if the will was strong enough. For those who cannot do it, constant awareness and resolve to do better will, over time, lessen and then break the pattern.

For instance, a hot temper is easier to control than a craving for sweets merely because the hot temper is easier to recognise and temper down when it arises, with all its disturbing emotions. Overeating or addictive behaviour patterns become chronically repetitive, because they were initially pleasurable and even now continue to be so.

For spiritual aspirants, the Katha Upanishad gives a clear choice: "The Good is one thing. The Pleasant is another." It is a matter of intention, for energy follows intention. No matter how many times you fail, try again. Take action instead of merely resolving to do so. If you are actually doing something that flows against the ingrained habit and also meditating, then, over time, the counter-flow will triumph over the bad habit. Pious wishes will not do. Action is imperative, as is clear thinking and patience.

The Buddha said, "Remove impurities from the self as does the silversmith – little by little, part by part, again and again."

Living a Balanced Life

What does it mean to 'live a balanced life'? How does one achieve such a balanced state of being?

Living a balanced life means living it with complete harmony of thought, feeling, and action that arises out of awareness. But how does awareness arise?

There are two aspects to the mind: the objective and the subjective.

You are related to the outside world through the objective mind, and the physical organ related to it is the brain. The objective mind is creative, and depends on what you think, feel and believe. It is the conscious mind and it responds to the stimulus from without, which may be in the form of pleasant and unpleasant sensations, depending on your thoughts. The conscious mind stands as a sentinel to the subconscious mind and when you 'sleep' it sleeps.

At the subtle level, the chakra related to it is the Ajna chakra. The Ajna chakra is the centre of discrimination, awareness and concentration.

You are connected to the world within through the subjective or the subconscious mind. It is believed that it occupies the whole physical body and, at the subtle level, the chakra related to it is the Manipura chakra.

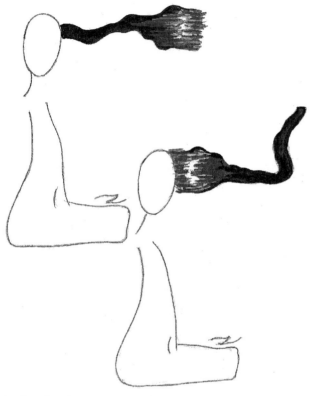

Developed and active Ajna chakra looking without and within.

The subjective mind is associated with sensations such as joy, imagination, fear, love, power, respiration and all other involuntary functions of the body. The efficient functioning of the subconscious mind entirely depends on the information supplied by the conscious mind. Depending on the clarity and authenticity of thought, the role of the subconscious mind is to manifest the result. Its work is ongoing and it does not 'sleep' when you sleep.

You may have observed that the structure of the two minds is the same i.e. the loops of the brain (objective mind) and the loops of the intestines, in the region of the solar plexus, are similar.

Manipura chakra awakens intensity and passion, essential for sound health and physical power. All positive thoughts expand this chakra and all negative thoughts contract it. The Manipura chakra has been likened to the sun because it is a central point of distribution for the energy through nerves all over the body.

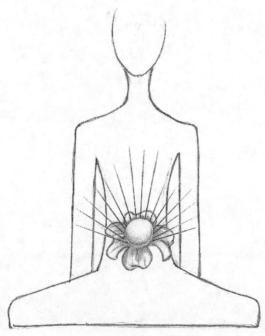

Flowering Manipura chakra.

Every thought is a cause and every condition an effect. For this reason it is essential that you control your thoughts so that only scrutinised data passes from the conscious to the subconscious mind. That would mean that the two hemispheres of the brain work in unison so that the subconscious mind brings forth desired results. Once, with practice, you learn to live in awareness from within, then the without will be a reflection of that.

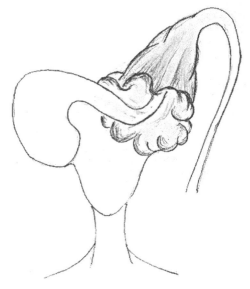

A mirror image of the left (logical) brain expanding to receive data from the right (creative) brain to bring about synchrony.

The secret to leading a balanced life is to understand the function and coordination of these two centres – the conscious (residing in the brain) and the subconscious (in the solar plexus) of our being.

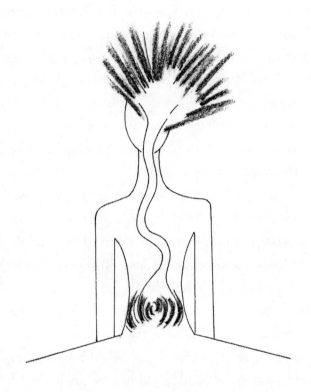

The fully operative Ajna chakra in complete coordination with Manipura chakra.

You need to understand that whatever the conscious mind accepts and decides as true, the subconscious automatically accepts as true without judgement. Once you realise this, you scrutinise every thought and after endorsing it with reason, allow it to pass through to the subconscious.

While the process of understanding the function and coordination between the two minds is going on, a simultaneous change occurs in the subtle body centres or chakras. In the process of living, you first think, then you feel, and then you act. The chakras that are responsible for this balance are Ajna chakra, Anahata chakra and Manipura chakra.

To ensure a better understanding, given below is an illustration showing the change that occurs in the chakras when balance and awareness is achieved in your thought process i.e. when thought, feeling and action support each other and move in harmony.

In the figure on the next page, you see that the Ajna chakra, which is the chakra of the conscious mind, extends and, clearing its way, passes through the Vishuddhi. The flowering of the Vishuddhi allows us to flow with life, allowing things to happen in the way they are happening. And so, accepting the dualities of life and harmonising of all opposites, it passes through the Anahata chakra, the centre for feeling, before moving into the Manipura chakra, collecting data on the way and moving back into the flowering Anahata chakra to assimilate and process the data collected in order to give an immediate access to all the wisdom. This might even extend much further to give access to subtler realms.

In this connection lies the power of the conscious mind. The subconscious will carry out any plan and idea suggested to it by the conscious mind. Hence the ability to manifest one's desires as well one's fears.

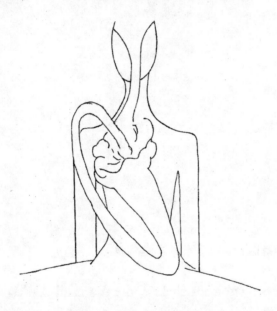

With the opening up of the Anahata chakra, one moves from expectation to unconditional love.

The awakened Ajna chakra and Manipura chakra.

When these two main chakras, the Ajna and the Manipura chakras, are brought into balance through awareness and practice (as seen in the above figures), then thought takes form and the law of creation will bring that thought into manifestation. You are free to choose what you think. The result of your thought is governed by this immutable law of creation. Therefore, it is essential that you cultivate the habit of constructive thinking.

When the seers of bygone days turned their gaze within for self-realisation, and to solve the riddle of the universe, they discovered that there is a vibrational grid on which the foundation of the physical body is based. They discovered that the major energy centres influence the corresponding organs in the physical body. They also found that in order for the human body, mind, and intellect to realise its full potential, the subtle chakras and nadis would have to be clear of all blocks created by negative thought patterns.

They realised that the three centres to fulfil this purpose were the Ajna chakra (the third eye), the Anahata chakra (the heart centre) and the Manipura chakra (the solar plexus). If these were balanced, then the human being could live a purposeful and meaningful life.

After contemplating on this discovery, the seers thought of a symbol that would enable the common man (who has no definite knowledge of cause and effect and is governed by his feelings and emotions) to function with some semblance of balance in his day-to-day life. They created the symbol of Ganpati in the manner in which the rishis experienced the expansion in their subtle body – an elongated Ajna chakra and an expanded Manipura chakra. The trunk of the Ganpati and the expanded belly draws the attention of an individual and with the focus on these two centres and corresponding mantras, he could unconsciously bring a balance to the intention with which he is going through the ritual of worship, resulting in the manifestation of his intent. Depending on his faith and sincerity of purpose during that period of focus, his thoughts, feelings and actions flow in a synchronised rhythm, thus producing the desired result.

When activated, the extended Ajna chakra will sometimes take the shape resembling that of Ganesha's trunk.

Lord Ganesha, the remover of all obstacles, is shown here
with his trunk curved to the left.

ACKNOWLEDGEMENTS

I wish to express, with love and joy, my deepest gratitude to:

My Guru, the late Justice M. L. Dudhat.

Master Charles Cannon for reading the manuscript and graciously writing the Foreword for it.

Suma Varughese and Goldy Makhijani for suggesting the 'Question-Answer' format for a book on Kundalini.

Rohit Arya for offering me the benefit of his wide-ranging experience and helping me provide in-depth answers to some of the more complex questions.

Shiv Sharma for his patience and unflagging attention to the editing of the manuscript.

Gautam, without whose commitment the book would not have become a reality.

My daughters Shibani and Nikki for their understanding and continued support.

Girish Jathar and Sanjay Malandkar for their efforts to bring the book to completion.

BIBLIOGRAPHY

Synchroncity newsletters, Master Charles Cannon, (Swami Vivekananda Saraswati).

Kundalini Tantra, Swami Satyananda Saraswati, Yoga Publications Trust, Munger, Bihar.

Prana Pranayama Prana Vidya, Swami Niranjanananananda Saraswati, Yoga Publications Trust, Munger, Bihar.

Kundalini Yoga, Volume 1, Osho, Sterling Publishers Pvt. Ltd., New Delhi.

Conscious Flight Into The Empyrean, Santosh Sachdeva, Yogi Impressions Books Pvt. Ltd., Mumbai.

Kundalini Diary, Santosh Sachdeva, Yogi Impressions Books Pvt. Ltd., Mumbai.

Kundalini Awakening, Santosh Sachdeva, Yogi Impressions Books Pvt. Ltd., Mumbai.

Meditation and Life, Swami Chinmayananda, Central Chinmaya Mission Trust, Mumbai.

Churning of the Heart, Swami Shivom Tirth, Devatma Shakti Society, Mumbra, Panvel Road, Thane.

The Second Dawn, Swami Shivom Tirth, Devatma Shakti Society, Mumbra, Panvel Road, Thane.

Kundalini, Evolution and Enlightenment, Edited by John White, Harper Collins Publishers, India.

The author may be contacted on email:
yogitosh@indiayogi.com

For further details, contact:
Yogi Impressions Books Pvt. Ltd.
1711, Centre 1, World Trade Centre,
Cuffe Parade, Mumbai 400 005, India.

Fill in the Mailing List form on our website
and receive, via email, information on
books, authors, events and more.
Visit: www.yogiimpressions.com

Telephone: (022) 22155036/7/8
Fax: (022) 22155039
E-mail: yogi@yogiimpressions.com

Also visit:
indiayōgi.
www.indiayogi.com

the complete spiritual e-shop

OTHER TITLES FROM SANTOSH SACHDEVA
PUBLISHED BY YOGI IMPRESSIONS

Conscious Flight into the Empyrean

A first-hand account of an extraordinary voyage into the subtle realms, this diary is a rare depiction of the visual unfolding of the Kundalini energy that challenges conventional views of perception and experience. It contains the author's own illustrations of the visions seen in her daily meditations.

Paperback, Colour

Kundalini Diary

So much fear-mongering has been generated in average literature about the Kundalini, that this book comes as a great relief in the assertion of another possibility. In this volume, the author shows that the arousal of Kundalini can be a natural process and not one to be dreaded. In fact, the Kundalini can become a good, wise and loving friend.

Paperback, Colour

Kundalini Awakening

One of the great merits of this book lies in its pointing out that the chakra or chakras which need activation will be energised first, even if apparently out of linear sequence. This is of immense significance as many people spend inordinate amounts of time worrying that the process has gone awry. This third volume in the Kundalini journey is full of experiences underwritten by a universal context. These are not Hindu or yogic, but universal.

Paperback, Colour

The Kundalini Trilogy

This set includes *Conscious Flight Into The Empyrean*, *Kundalini Diary* and *Kundalini Awakening*. The three Kundalini books are a first hand account describing, in vivid detail, the author's extraordinary journey into the subtle realms. Accompanied by her own illustrations of the visions seen in daily meditations, they are in the form of a daily journal written in a simple language that the reader can identify with easily.

Paperback, Colour